WHEN LOVE AIN'T ENOUGH

A NOVEL

STACEY COVINGTON-LEE

Copyright © 2017 – Stacey Covington-Lee

This is a work of fiction and is not meant to depict, portray, or represent any particular person. Names, characters, places, and incidents are either the product of the author's imagination or are used fictitiously. Any resemblances to an actual person, living or dead, is entirely coincidental.

All rights reserved. No part of this publication may be reproduced, stored in or introduced into any retrieval system or transmitted in any form or by any means (electronic, mechanical, photocopying, recording, or otherwise) without prior written permission of the copyright owner.

ISBN-13: 978-0-692-82857-1

Edited by: Tamara Grant
Book Cover:
Formatting/Typesetting: Allyson Edits
Printed in the United States of America

DEDICATION

This is dedicated to my forever friend, my "ride or die," Cassandra Renee Smith and to my older sister, T'Irma Covington. T'Irma, I'm writing these stories for us and soon I'll tell yours. Rest in sweet peace, Schmitty and Sister.

ACKNOWLEDGEMENTS

First and foremost, I'd like to thank my Heavenly Father for all that He has done for me. I recognize that this is a gift from Him and I promise to honor that gift and work to make it better with each book I write.

Thank you to my beautiful family for all of the love and support that you continue to give me. Thank you to my husband, Kenneth Lee, for helping me realize this dream. I thank you and our son, Joshua Lee, for every encouraging word, for tolerating the late nights, book events, and travel time. I know that hanging out and watching me chat with readers isn't always fun for you guys, but thank you for your willingness to do it and the smiles with which you do it. I love you both so very much.

When I think about all of the readers that have supported me, left reviews, in boxed me, commented on posts regarding my books, and come out to events, my heart gets full. Thank you to each and every person that has ever read my work. I absolutely love writing, but your positive feedback and knowing that you all are waiting to read the next book makes the writing experience even more pleasurable. I promise to always give you quality reading material and I will strive to make the next book better than the last book. Thank you to all of the book clubs and radio shows that have hosted me and helped spread the word about my work. I recognize that you all play a monumental role in the success of my books and I thank you.

A special thank you to Tamara Grant of CLS26 Media for all that you do. You are a joy to work with and I appreciate everything you've done from editing to public relations. This has been a partnership made in literary heaven. Thank you to Allyson Deese of Allyson Edits for the amazing book cover and your typesetting/formatting services. You've been an absolute joy to work with. Last but certainly not least, I'd like to thank Keonna Whipple for being my reviewer, my sounding board, and my friend. You are greatly appreciated.

PART I
THE DECONSTRUCTION OF LOVE

CHAPTER ONE

"Really Vince, how stupid do you have to be to not know that you need to bring home all of your receipts so that they can be entered into the checkbook? I mean at what point does common sense kick in? Or am I assuming too much by believing that you actually have an ounce of common sense?"

"Roz, I have no idea what the hell you're talking about," Vince sighed deeply as he closed the front door behind him.

The screeching of her mother's voice drew Lisa out of her room. "Mama, what are you yelling about?"

"Your dumb ass father neglected to bring home the receipt for the Starbucks he had the other day, and now it's thrown the checkbook all out of balance. I mean damn, how hard can it be to log your expenses."

"Why do you have to speak to him like that? He's a man, your husband, not some little boy who's been misbehaving. Talk to him with some respect," Lisa demanded.

Vince walked up to his youngest daughter and gave her a sweet peck on the cheek. "Daddy loves you baby, but I don't want you to get involved. I can fight my own battles. Go on back in your room and finish studying. That nursing exam is no joke and I want you to be well prepared."

"Okay Daddy. I love you." Lisa turned to head back down the hall, but not before throwing her mother an ugly glare. One that warned her to leave her dad alone.

Looking weary, Vince slowly walked into the family room and plopped down in his comfortable chair. He leaned forward and rubbed his hands over his head in frustration.

All he'd wanted was to come home to a quiet house and a good meal. He couldn't remember the last time he'd walked into the house and was greeted warmly by his wife. He couldn't understand how the years had turned her so bitter and mean. He loved her now just as he always had, but clearly, her love was changing as the years were rolling by. He still bought her flowers, wrote her love letters, and told her how beautiful she was. She'd always loved his sweet, sentimental, romantic side. Now it just seemed to annoy her. He continued to rub his head as he thought about the woman she used to be.

They met twenty-four years ago, when she was an innocent and beautiful nineteen-year-old girl. Vince was visiting family when Rozalla and a couple of other girls walked in with one of his cousins. He was so taken with her beauty that he could hardly speak. She had the most beautiful golden skin, long wavy hair and a smile that could melt an iceberg. Her Latin and African American heritage had blessed her with the body of a goddess. Rozalla was the most perfect thing Vince had ever seen. At the time, he was a twenty-one year old, tall, lanky mechanic's apprentice that didn't think he was at all good enough for the likes of Rozalla. But to his great delight, she smiled at him and later told his cousin that she thought he was handsome. Ten months later, they stood before a small gathering of family and friends and vowed to love, respect and honor each other for the rest of their lives. Within the first three years of marriage, they'd had two beautiful daughters. He'd managed to land a job as a mechanic with a large dealership, and she'd struggled through nursing school. It wasn't always easy, but they'd found their sweet spot. They laughed together, respectfully worked through any issues, kept the romantic fires burning, and demonstrated to their girls what true love was all about. Then it all changed.

Heather Ramos was the name that Vince regrets ever hearing. She's the woman that Rozalla met, befriended, and allowed to plant seeds of doubt in her head about their love and happiness. After two months of knowing Heather, Rozalla decided that nothing they had was good enough, the trips they took weren't grand enough, and Vince himself was no longer man enough for her. That was two years ago and since then living with Rozalla was almost unbearable. Making her happy was impossible.

"Are you even listening to me?" Rozalla screamed as she pounded her fist on the small end table. "I asked you a question and you're sitting there like some mute."

The shrill of her voice abruptly ended Vince's journey down memory lane. "I'm sorry baby, what did you ask me?"

"Did you ask your boss for that raise we talked about?"

"Roz, they just gave me a promotion and a raise three months ago. It's completely unrealistic to think that I'm going to get another raise before next year's annual review. Baby, we're doing great right now, why are you concerned about me getting another raise?"

"If I've told you once, I've told you a thousand times, I want a new car. I really want that new Infiniti Q70. If you ask for a raise then there would be no reason for me to not get it."

"You can't be serious? Your Maxima isn't even two years old. You begged me for that car and I gladly bought it for you. I'm not buying any more cars any time soon," Vince explained.

"I swear, you're so damn mean. You just don't want to see me happy."

"How could you possibly say that with a straight face? I break my back for you and our girls every day. I do the very best that I can to make sure that you all have everything you need, and most of what you want. What else could I possibly do to make you happy?"

"You can drop dead. You'd be worth more to me then, and I could even afford my car," she said with an evil glimmer in her eye.

Rozalla's words cut like a knife. Vince got up from his chair, went to their bedroom, showered and dressed for bed. He no longer had an appetite; it had been replaced with a headache and a deep heartache. He never imagined he'd hear such cruel words ever cross his sweet Roz's lips. What happened to the woman he'd married? Had everything they'd built meant nothing to her? When had she become so weak-minded that some silly friend could persuade her that life would be better with more material possessions? Or would her life really be better without him? All of the questions rolling through his head sent pains through his chest. All he wanted was to love his wife and be loved in return.

A few hours later, Rozalla headed for bed. "Great, now I have to listen to his snoring," she complained as she laid beside her husband. She didn't snuggle up to him like she used to do, but instead turned her back to him and eventually drifted off.

Six a.m. rolled around so fast. The blaring alarm snatched Rozalla from her slumber. "Vince, hit the alarm," she mumbled. However, Vince didn't move fast enough for her so she reached over him and shut it off. "Vince, come on and get up now or you'll be late for work." She nudged him, but he still didn't wake up. Panic started to set in. "Vince, get up, get up!" But all the screaming and shaking in the world wouldn't wake Vince. He was dead.

CHAPTER TWO

So many people had been coming and going all day. Some bringing flowers, others arriving with a variety of food items, and some empty-handed, but with plenty of well wishes and expressions of sympathy. This undoubtedly had been the longest, hardest day of Rozalla's life. After the last guest had been shown out, she plopped down at the kitchen table, unable to recall what the majority of visitors had said. Her head was in a dense fog and she wasn't sure when it would be clear again.

"Are you okay, Roz? Why don't you let me help you into bed?" Amanda asked. She'd observed her best friend all day, she knew how disconnected Rozalla was from the world right now. Aside from Vincent, Amanda knew Rozalla better than anyone. They'd been best friends since seventh grade. Amanda was there when Rozalla and Vincent met; she was the matron of honor at their wedding and Rozalla's closest confidant. "Honey, you are in a daze and need to rest. Tomorrow is going to be a very difficult day and you'll need to be well rested, both mentally and physically to get through it," Amanda warned.

"Oh, she'll get through it just fine, won't you Mama?" Lisa asked with a nasty tone to her voice.

"Lisa, why would you say something like that to Mama?" Carmen quizzed as she walked through the door. Carmen was their oldest daughter and had rushed back to town as soon as she received word of her father's passing.

"Let her tell you, Carmen. Let Mama tell you how none of this is difficult for her; it's just what she wanted. I bet she can't wait to drop Daddy in his grave so that she can dance on top of it. Isn't that right, Mama?" Lisa's words dripped with venom.

Everyone looked completely shocked and confused; that is, everyone but Rozalla. She looked angry and didn't hesitate to jump out of her chair, march over to her youngest and slap her across her pretty little face. "How could you speak to me like that? What in the world is wrong with you?" Rozalla screamed.

"I'm speaking to you the same way you spoke to Daddy, when you told him that he could make you happy by dropping dread! Remember that? Those were the last words you ever spoke to him. That was the last thing he heard before he closed his eyes and died. Your evil, greedy words are what killed him," Lisa sobbed.

Hearing her words thrown back in her face was like being doused with gasoline and set on fire. Rozalla fell to the floor and cried like a wounded animal. Her sobs were uncontrollable. Knowing that Vincent had left this world thinking that she truly wished him dead was more than she could take. What had she done? Did her husband really pass away because of the evil words she'd said? Had he died of a broken heart? She cried for what seemed like an eternity and despite Carmen and Amanda's best efforts, they weren't able to get her off of the floor and calm her down. Her sobs and moans went on for the better part of an hour. Finally, when Lisa managed to muster up some compassion and kneel at her mother's side, Rozalla calmed down. She'd whispered something into her mother's ear, kissed her forehead and convinced her to get up and go to bed.

A little while later, Carmen returned to the kitchen, where Lisa was still seated. Carmen watched as her baby sister mindlessly pinched off tiny pieces of cake and tossed them in her mouth.

"Keep on and those tiny bites are going to be the equivalent of half the cake. Next thing you know you'll be dieting, trying to figure out where the extra weight came from," Carmen warned as she took a seat.

"I wouldn't care, right now I don't care about a thing," Lisa replied somberly.

"Those were some pretty harsh words you said to Mama. Think you may have gone overboard? I know she can say some ugly things, but you exaggerating her statement right now isn't at all helpful."

"That's just it, Carmen, I didn't exaggerate a thing. Every word I said, the quote that I repeated was completely true. You see how she reacted, that alone should've told you that I wasn't making any of it up. That and the fact that we are always honest with each other. You know I don't go around spreading lies, or purposefully causing tension just for the hell of it."

"Why would she be so mean and nasty to Daddy?"

"I told you months ago, ever since she befriended that Heather chick, nothing Daddy did or said was good enough. All she's done is bitch and moan at him mercilessly. I don't see how he was able to keep himself from snapping on her. I'm telling you, Carmen, she'd been downright evil."

Carmen stood and walked over to the sink, where she dropped her head and let her tears fall freely. The thought of her sweet, kind, generous, loving father being mistreated was heartbreaking. But for that treatment to come from the woman he loved most was almost unbearable.

"I know how you're feeling," Lisa whispered as she walked to the sink and gently rubbed her big sister's shoulder.

"No you don't," Carmen sniffed. "Maybe if I hadn't moved away, I would've been able to keep Mom from straying so far from the woman we know her to be."

"Oh please, Carmen. You only moved an hour away and unless you were prepared to knock off this Heather chick, I don't think you would've prevented any of this. Besides, you know how proud Dad was of you opening your own salon. He thought it was genius to open it on UGA property. I don't know of anyone else that's been able to lease space on a college campus like that. And now look at you, almost every female in Athens comes to your salon," Lisa boasted. The admiration she had for her big sister was undeniable.

A big smile crept across Carmen's face, but before she could utter a word, the doorbell rang. Her smile soured as she asked, "Now who would wait this late to come over?"

The girls walked to the door together and when Carmen opened it, there stood a tall, voluptuous, Latina woman. Her hair flowed down her back and while she was attractive, she would've been more beautiful had her makeup not been overdone. "May I help you?" Carmen quizzed.

The woman stepped forward, but then Lisa stepped forward and blocked her path. "What do you want?"

"I'm so sorry to hear about your father, sweetie. I'm here to see your mother and offer my help. I'm sure she needs a friend right now," the woman answered sympathetically.

Lisa rolled her eyes in disgust. "Heather, my mother has all the friends and moral support she needs. Besides, it's late and she's tired. I'll be sure and let her know you stopped by." Lisa proceeded to close the door in the woman's face as she pleaded for the chance to see Rozalla. Lisa locked the door and returned to the kitchen.

"So that's Heather? She looks like a cheap, Sofia Vergara wanna-be. I don't understand how Mom even came to be friends with her."

"I don't know, but I hope that Mama now realizes that Heather is not the kind of friend she needs. She's an influence that needs to stay far, far away," Lisa commented. "But enough of this, I'm tired and going to bed. I don't know how much sleep I'll get knowing that we'll lay our father to rest tomorrow, but I've got to try for a couple of hours rest."

"All right, Lisa, sleep well. I'm going to check on Mom and then head to bed myself. I love you."

"Love you too."

Carmen straightened up the kitchen and was about to head to bed when Amanda walked in to announce her departure for the night. "Do you mind letting me out, Carmen? I'm going to head home for a few hours, but I'll be back first thing in the morning."

"Of course I'll see you out," Carmen replied. As she went to open the front door, Carmen turned and looked Amanda straight in the eye. "I want to thank you, Amanda. Thank you for being here for my mom, for remaining her true friend and supporting her the way that you have. It really means a lot to all of us."

"It's my pleasure and like the song says, that's what friends are for," Amanda smiled sweetly and headed out the door, jumped in her car and was gone.

Carmen stood in the door-way for a couple of minutes, and let the cool breeze of the night wash over her. She looked up and down the street and wondered if any of the other neighborhood families were experiencing the kind of heartbreak that they were right now. Were they in mourning or was that god-awful experience reserved just for the Harper family? She wiped a couple of tears from her cheeks, closed and locked the door, turned off the lights and headed towards the bedrooms. Her mother's door was slightly cracked and she decided to peek in and make sure that Roz was okay. All looked well, but as she started to close the door back, she heard her mom whisper her name.

"Carmen, come on in for a minute please."

"I thought you were asleep. You know you really need to try and get some shut eye. Tomorrow is going to be a hard day and I don't need you collapsing from grief and exhaustion."

Rozalla sniffed and wiped tears. "This bed is so big without your father in it. I can't sleep alone. Please lay down with me until I drift off."

Despite what Lisa had told her about their mother's behavior, Carmen's heart still broke for her. She'd just lost the only man she'd ever loved, her companion for the past twenty-three years. She not only had to deal with his passing, but the enormous guilt she carried had to be overwhelming. Without saying a word, Carmen laid down on her father's side of the bed. Her face in his pillow, she inhaled his scent and cried more silent tears. It wasn't long before she and her mother cried themselves to sleep.

CHAPTER THREE

The house was starting to fill with family as the hour of the funeral services approached. Lisa refused to wear anything black. Her father's life was more vibrant than black, so she chose to celebrate his life by wearing a beautiful white dress, with a purple ribbon tied delicately around her waist. After all, purple was Vincent's favorite color. Carmen entered the living room wearing a lovely lilac dress. She too was mindful of her father's favorite color and the fact that he wouldn't want everything and everyone dark and dreary. Then entered Rozalla and lo and behold, she was dressed in all black, from the ridiculous veil covering her face to the hideous shoes on her feet. The girls looked at one another as if to ask, *'what the hell is she thinking?'* Rozalla could feel her daughters' eyes burrowing a hole through her, but she chose to ignore their obvious disgust with her choice of attire. But her clothing was a true representation of how she was feeling...dark. There was no part of her that felt alive, no part of her soul that felt she deserved to be vibrant as she honored the memory of Vincent. After all, she was the cause of his death. No matter how many times she'd been told he had a heart attack, she knew in her heart that it was her evil ways that stopped his heart from beating.

"Mama, are you sure that this is what you want to wear?" Carmen whispered in her mom's ear as she gently placed her hands on her shoulders. "You know how Dad loved you in yellow and pink. Wouldn't you like to change into something that's a little more colorful?"

"No, I deserve to wear this black. The way I treated your father these last couple of years, it was wrong, it was mean, and it was evil. I won't stand here now dressed like a breath of fresh air, when in reality, I was the darkness that suffocated him."

"Don't you think you're being a tad dramatic?" Lisa asked as she walked up behind her mother.

"My husband is gone and as you so eloquently put it, I killed him. So no, I don't think I'm being dramatic, I think I'm owning up to the wrong that I've done. And quite frankly, I thought that would make you happy."

"Wrong again, Mom, nothing about any of this makes me happy. My daddy is gone and happiness is an emotion that I can't even recognize right now."

The front door opened and the funeral director entered with of couple of his staff members. He instructed everyone to gather in a circle and hold hands as he led them in prayer. After all the Amen's were echoed, the family was ushered out to the waiting limousine and everyone else was given a funeral sticker for their car, and instructed to ride in the processional with their headlights on. As they approached the church, they were blown away by the number of cars in the parking lot, and the multitude of mourners waiting to enter the sanctuary. Regardless of what his wife had thought of him in recent years, Vincent was loved and respected by many. The eulogy was beautiful, truthful and poignant. It wasn't just a minister delivering random words, but a man honoring his friend. Vincent and Minister Jacobs had become close years ago when Vincent had stepped up to lead a youth group of young boys. Minister Jacobs admired how Vincent had gained the respect of the boys. He was amazed at how stern he was, yet sensitive and encouraging. He'd changed the lives of many, and the love that people felt for him reached far beyond the youth group.

The service went on longer than expected, because of the multitude of people that wanted to speak of Vincent's kindness. Their tributes were overwhelming and the brief grave side prayer and interment was emotionally draining. The family was taken back to the church for the repast where they were well fed and the recipients of more condolences. While all of the kind words and gestures were appreciated, Lisa wanted nothing more than to get back to the peace and solitude of their home. Looking at her mother soak up all the attention as if this were her moment to shine was absolutely nauseating.

"You okay over here, little sis? The look on your face says that you're not," Carmen observed.

"Look at her, Carmen. She actually looks like she's enjoying herself. I mean forgive me if I'm wrong, but all of this attention being showered on her is bringing her joy. Never mind the reason for the attention, that's no real concern for her. Just the fact that she's in the spotlight is all that's important to her."

"Don't you think you're being a little harsh, Lisa?"

"Look over there at her now, Carmen, and then tell me I'm being too harsh," Lisa nodded in her mother's direction. Rozalla was dabbing at her eyes, that were bone dry by the way, all while leaning over with her head resting on the big, strong shoulder of Minister Jacobs. She'd finally taken that ridiculous veil off, and was playing the role of the grieving widow, all while finding new ways and reasons to touch the chest of the good minister.

"Still think I'm being harsh?" Lisa asked.

"It's time for us to go!" Carmen marched over to her mother, grabbed her by the arm and insisted that they leave. "You've put on enough of a show, now it's time to leave. Amanda is waiting to take us home. Let's go!"

"What is wrong with you?" Rozalla growled. "Can I at least do the decent thing and tell everyone thank you and goodbye?"

Minister Jacobs interjected, "I'll gladly address the congregation on your behalf. You all head on out and try and get some rest. It's been a long, difficult day and some quiet time would serve you well."

Rozalla looked annoyed with both the minister and her daughter, but decided to go ahead and leave without any further objections. Amanda, Rozalla, Carmen, and Lisa rode home in complete silence. But once they were in the house, the fireworks started.

"Now why don't you all tell me why you dragged me out of the repast like that? I was having a good conversation with Minister Jacobs about how I'm going to go on without the love of my life. He was comforting me!"

Lisa slammed her purse on the table and spoke through clenched teeth. "You were carrying on like some two-bit whore. You couldn't wait to start groping the minister. For goodness sake, he was one of Daddy's best friends. I honestly don't understand why Daddy was ever attracted to you, or how he managed to stay in love with your trashy ass as long as he did."

"You will not stand in my house and talk to me like that! Who in the hell do you think you are? You are the child, not me, and as long as you live in my house, you will talk to me and treat me with the respect that I deserve," Rozalla demanded.

"You couldn't pay me to stay here with you. I'll be out by the first of the week," Lisa promised as she walked out of the room.

"Do you feel the same way your sister does?" Rozalla asked Carmen in almost a whisper of a voice.

"Mama, I don't understand you right now. You did behave disrespectfully and it made everyone around you uncomfortable. Daddy deserved more from you than the behavior you exhibited today. While the service itself was nice, you personally did nothing to honor Daddy. Can you imagine how hurt he would be if he'd seen you flirting with his best friend? For you to use his funeral to gain attention for yourself and throw yourself at the minister was beyond disgraceful. I swear, I don't even know who you are any more. You need to do some soul searching and bring back the amazing mother that we once knew and the woman that Daddy fell in love with." Carmen fished her keys out of her purse, wiped the tears from her eyes, and left.

"Go ahead Amanda, take your best shot at me. Tell me how awful I've been." Rozalla braced herself for the harsh words that she knew were dangling on her best friend's lips. But the words never came. Instead, Amanda kissed her on the cheek and left.

Rozalla stood alone in her living room, thinking of how she'd carried on. It was disgraceful and she felt ashamed. Vince would have been so hurt to see her acting the way she had earlier. She was an embarrassment to his memory, his legacy. She looked at her outfit, thought of her behavior, and decided that she needed to get back to the person that he'd fallen in love with, back to the respectable woman he'd admired.

CHAPTER FOUR

Six months had passed since her husband's death, and Rozalla had come to know just how lonely being a widow could be. Lisa had moved out, just as she'd vowed she would. Carmen was back in Athens and didn't make the short trip to Atlanta to visit her as often as she used to. They were both still angry over her behavior at their father's funeral. She'd apologized, but her words seemed to have fallen on deaf ears. Amanda was still being the true friend that she always was, but she couldn't be there every day to ask Rozalla how her day was, share dinner or keep her warm at night. Rozalla was missing Vince more and more with the passing of each day. Heather had tried to get her to go out a few times, but after the funeral fiasco, Rozalla had limited her activities to work and home. She'd been a virtual hermit for the past few months and she was lonely.

The phone rang and Rozalla immediately walked towards it, hoping that it would be someone with some good, entertaining conversation. "Hello."

"What are you doing right now?" Heather quizzed.

"Feeling sorry for myself. What about you, what have you been up to today?"

"Let me tell you about my day over drinks. Get dressed and I'll swing by and pick you up. We could both use a little time away from home."

"Now Heather, you already know that I'm not going anywhere. Well, I take that back, I am going to run out to Publix for a few items and then grab some Popeye's chicken for a five-star meal," Rozalla said jokingly.

"No you're not! Roz, I'm tired of you punishing yourself over Vince. No, you shouldn't have said some of the things that you said to him, and yes, you could've handled yourself better at his funeral. But that's all over now and being miserable isn't going to change any of it. You know good and well that Vince wouldn't want you to be this unhappy."

"Heather, it's easy for you to say all of that and I appreciate your trying to make me feel better about things, but…"

"Stop it," Heather interrupted. "You've got to stop punishing yourself. Seriously, enough is enough. Now you can either get dressed, or I can come over and dress you, but either way you're going out with me tonight. It's Friday and there's a couple of martinis somewhere with our names on them. So get ready and I'll see you in an hour."

Heather hung up before Rozalla could get her rebuttal out. So instead, she hung up the phone, took a deep breath, and headed for her closet. As she flipped through the clothes, it seemed as if there was nothing decent in there. Then she smiled to herself as she heard Vince's voice say "Baby, you look good in whatever you put on. Now pick something and let's go." Yes, he'd said that every single time that they went out. He actually thought that it made her hurry along. Then she spotted a floral dress that he used to love to see her in. It stopped a couple of inches above the knee and fit her curves like a glove. He thought it was sexy without being sleazy. So she pulled it out, laid it on the bed and headed for the shower. Forty-five minutes later the doorbell rang and Rozalla was ready to go.

"I thought we were going out for a drink?" Rozalla was puzzled as Heather pulled up to the valet at the W Hotel.

"We are, there is a great bar up on the top floor. It's pretty popular too and plenty of gorgeous men come through for their happy hour."

"I'm here for the drinks, not the men," Rozalla announced very matter-of-factly.

"We'll see," Heather smirked as she stepped out of the car.

Heather, with her long, lean body, thick, wavy hair and striking looks, grabbed her fair share of attention as soon as they'd walked in. It was nothing however, compared to the attention that was focused on Rozalla. Yes, she was forty-three with adult children, but she didn't look a day over thirty and her curvaceous body was the kind that men drooled over. As they took a seat at the bar, Rozalla began to pull on her dress a little bit. The stares had her concerned that it may have been too short or too tight. Vince had always loved her in it, but he was her husband, and it was okay for him to look at her with lustful eyes.

"Stop fidgeting with your clothes," Heather fussed. "You look like some nervous school girl."

"Then I look exactly how I feel. I'm really feeling as if it were too soon for me to be going out like this. I'm not ready for this kind of scene."

"Number one, people don't use the word *scene* like that anymore and number two, you're far too attractive and lonely to stay cooped up in the house, all night every night. Now what do you want to drink?"

"You and that mouth of yours are going to get on my nerves, Heather."

"Yeah, yeah, whatever. What are you drinking, girl?"

"I don't know, something fruity I guess. Ooh, something like a sex on the beach," Rozalla said with a little excitement in her voice. "Vince used to get those for me back in the day when we'd go out with friends."

"The key words there were *back in the day*. Please allow me to usher you into the twenty-first century." Heather turned to the bartender and ordered them a couple pomegranate martinis.

"Umm, this is good," Rozalla admitted. "I'm ashamed to admit that I'd never even heard of this drink. I mean I'd heard of a martini, but not a flavored one like this. Vince and I had our standard drinks and we just didn't ever stray away from them."

"Please don't be offended by this, Roz, but Vince is gone and you're going to have to start living for yourself and experiencing new things," Heather advised. "Don't get me wrong, I know you can't forget twenty-three years of marriage overnight, but you're going to have to open yourself up to new opportunities and experiences."

"Don't get me wrong, Heather, but regardless of the new experiences, I will never forget my years with Vince. He was a wonderful man that loved his family. He treated me like a queen, loved me deeply, and wanted nothing more than to make me happy. I just hate that I was too stupid to realize it when he was here." Rozalla picked up a cocktail napkin and dabbed the tears from her eyes.

"I'm sorry, Rozalla, I didn't mean to upset you. I know that Vince was a good man and I never meant to insinuate that you should forget all that you two shared."

"Okay," Rozalla sniffed. "Let's start this evening over. How was your day today? Is your new boss still being a jackass?"

Heather had recently taken a new position with a home health nursing agency. She was responsible for hiring the nursing staff and matching them with clients. She had replaced the man who'd held that position since the company started. To say that her supervisor had a strong bond with him was a monumental understatement. From what other employees had shared with Heather; Patrick, her supervisor, and the guy she replaced golfed together on the weekends. Their families vacationed together and they gladly lied for one another to cover up affairs that they were both involved in. Patrick was devastated when his partner in crime decided to leave for a better opportunity, and now he overly scrutinized every little thing that Heather did.

"Girl, being an ass is the only way he knows how to be. Now that he's finally stopped harassing me about every decision I make, he's decided to start making sexual advances."

"Are you serious?"

"Yes, I'm totally serious," Heather said as she tossed her hair over her shoulder. "He's always telling me that I have kissable shoulders. Constantly asking me if my man is keeping me happy. All kinds of foolishness like that, girl. He's annoying as all hell."

Rozalla took a long sip of her drink as she contemplated her next question. Heather had been known to sleep with co-workers in the past, and Rozalla wanted to know if that might be the case now. "So I know you say he's annoying, but how does he look and have you entertained any of his advances?"

"Are you seriously asking me that?"

"Oh please, don't act all offended. It's not like you haven't had the occasional office affair. You've said yourself how exciting they can be," Rozalla blurted out.

"Humph, I did say that, didn't I? In that case, he is pretty cute and has a nice body. Makes me wonder how his wife manages to hold on to him, because she's a frumpy old thing. She's a solid size sixteen, only wears her hair in a tight bun, and seems to live in sweats. If she knew what I knew, she'd spruce herself up. Get that hair done, slap on some make-up, and for the love of God, put on some decent clothes."

"Bless her heart. Maybe she doesn't feel good about herself because of the weight, or maybe the kids are driving her crazy."

"Bull crap, Rozalla. There are some sexy, plus-sized women and they have a dog. For reasons unknown, she was never able to conceive. So there is absolutely no reason that she can't dress up for her man. She's stupid for sending her man out into corporate America with all these beautiful women and not make sure she's all dolled up when he gets home."

"I don't know Heather, it's easy to say all of these things about the woman when you don't know the inner workings of their relationship. Not being able to have a baby, his cheating, maybe she feels that getting dolled up for him is a waste of her time."

"But you getting dolled up wasn't a waste. You look gorgeous," a random voice commented from behind Rozalla.

"Excuse me?" Rozalla asked, as she swung around with annoyance in her voice. But when her eyes met with those of the man behind her, she was dumbstruck. He was an incredibly handsome man.

"I'm sorry, I didn't mean to upset you, but you are so beautiful. I couldn't allow myself to walk by without speaking."

"You didn't upset her," Heather interjected. "She just didn't realize you were back there. Hi, I'm Heather, and this is my friend, Rozalla." Heather extended her hand as she waited for him to say his name.

Instead of taking Heather's hand, the stranger extended his hand towards Rozalla. "Hello, I'm Corbin."

Rozalla hesitantly extended her hand. "It's nice to meet you," she said bashfully. She was still in awe of how attracted she was to him. Then her mind flashed to Vince and she snatched her hand back and diverted her eyes.

"I'm sorry, did I squeeze your hand too tightly?"

"No, I just realized that my husband wouldn't be too happy with my holding on to another man's hand."

"I meant no disrespect, I just wanted to pay my compliments to the most beautiful woman I've seen in a very long time. Please tell your husband that he's a very lucky man."

"She's actually a widow," Heather interjected.

Corbin turned his attention back to Rozalla. "I'm sorry to hear that, you're far too young to have had to endure the loss of a spouse. I won't intrude on your time anymore, but when you think you're ready to entertain a little conversation, please give me a call," he said as he passed her his business card. "Good night ladies," he smiled as he turned and walked away.

"Let me see that," Heather demanded as she snatched the card out of Rozalla's hand. "Oh hell, this dude is the president of a law firm. Handsome and successful, I know it's a little soon for you, Roz, but you may want to give him a chance. I know you're tired of all those lonely nights."

"Lonely or not, it's too soon for me to be entertaining another man. My husband's only been gone six months, he deserves more respect than that."

"No disrespect, but exactly how long do you think is the appropriate mourning time? How long will you have to be lonely and alone? Most importantly, do you think that Vince would want you to be lonely and alone?"

"This is new to me, Heather. I don't know what the proper time is, I just know it seems soon and I know that people will talk negatively if it gets out that I'm dating. Of course Vince would never want me to be lonely. He loved me too much to want me to be miserable."

"Then to hell with what people think. No one has to live in your skin or with your decisions but you. So I say write your number down and give it to Corbin. Nothing may come of it except good conversation, but even that's better than talking to the walls."

Rozalla grew quite as she mulled over what her friend had just said. She was right, no one has to live with her decisions but her. No one is in that house but her and no one has to live that loneness but her. She loved Vince so much and didn't want to do anything to disrespect his memory or what they had. Unfortunately, the fact of the matter was he was no longer here. Rozalla ordered another drink and tossed it back without hesitation. She reached in her purse for a pen and wrote her number on the back of the card Corbin had given her. She spotted him across the room, strutted over to him and gave him his card back. "Feel free to call me sometime."

She didn't wait for a reply, she just walked back to Heather, grabbed her purse, paid her tab and they left.

CHAPTER FIVE

"Wait, you're doing what?" Amanda yelled into the phone. "I know I didn't hear you right. For a second I thought you said you were going out on a date."

"You heard me right," Rozalla replied defiantly.

"Your husband has only been gone a hot minute! Do you really think that you're prepared to move on after all those years of marriage? I mean it's not like you got a divorce, your husband died." Amanda had gotten up from her desk and was pacing back and forth across the floor, something she often did when she was frustrated.

"Don't you think I know better than anyone that my husband died? I'm reminded of it every day that I go home to an empty house, and every night that I crawl in that empty bed. And I loved my husband dearly, but he is no longer here."

The last couple of years had left Amanda confused about Rozalla's behavior, her attitude towards Vince, and her new-found friendship with Heather. Lisa had tried to tell her that Heather was a horrible influence on her mother, but Amanda refused to believe that a grown ass woman could be that easily influenced. Apparently she was wrong and Lisa had been right all along. Now Amanda was left trying to figure out how to get Rozalla to slow down and not step out into the dating scene so soon. Whether she realized it or not, she needed more time to mourn, more time to heal.

"Are you still there?" Rozalla inquired.

"Yes, I'm here. When is this date and who are you going out with?"

"It's tonight, with a guy named Corbin. I met him last week when I went out for drinks with Heather."

Amanda plopped back down in her chair and dropped her head on her desk. "I should've known," she mumbled.

"What did you say?"

"Nothing, I'm just surprised. I was calling to try and get you to go out to dinner with me. This was the last thing I expected to hear. Is it okay with you if I come over while you get ready for this date?"

"Sure," Rozalla conceded. "If meeting him will make you feel better, then you just bring your little self on over. He's picking me up at eight."

"Fine, I'll be there by six. Bye."

Amanda hung up the phone and ran her hands through her hair in frustration. She was convinced that Rozalla had no idea what she was getting into. Shame on that damn Heather for pushing her away from her husband and now pushing her into situations that she's not ready for. Amanda, as a medical office manager, submitted the last few claims that she had for the day. It wasn't long before she shut down her computer, grabbed her belongings and left for Rozalla's house. Amanda wasn't fazed by the traffic, she was too busy worrying about how she would try and get Rozalla to see that this dating thing was too much too soon.

Trying to mentally prepare herself for the conversation that she knew was coming, Rozalla walked into the kitchen and poured herself a glass of liquid courage. She walked with her wine glass back down the hall to her bedroom and started searching through the clothes in her closet. She yanked out outfit after outfit and nothing seemed appropriate. The items that were stylish were too sexy for a first date. The things that weren't sexy seemed frumpy. She plopped down on the bed, turned her wine glass up to her lips, and didn't pull it back down until it was empty. *'Maybe I should pour another glass,'* she thought, and immediately talked herself out of it. Rozalla didn't want to enter the dating arena tipsy. She needed to be able to think clearly, hold intelligent conversation, and be sure that Corbin was someone that she'd want to spend more time with. She got up to resume her search for the perfect outfit when she heard the doorbell ring. She quickly padded down the hall, anxious to have Amanda help her find something nice to wear.

"Hola chica, come on in," Rozalla greeted her friend with a big smile and open arms.

"Hey yourself, aren't you mighty bubbly today?" Amanda commented as she pulled away from the tight hug that Rozalla had wrapped her in. "So is this what you plan on wearing and if so, has this date been turned into a slumber party?"

"You're such a wise ass. No, I will not be wearing my bathrobe and I've only met him once, so there are absolutely no plans for a slumber party, sleep over and anything else that might lead to intense physical contact."

"Well I guess I should be glad for that."

"What's that supposed to mean, Amanda?"

"It means that as hard as I've tried, I can't wrap my mind around your deciding to date so soon after Vince's passing. I know you're lonely, but do you really feel like you're ready for all of this?" Amanda asked as she gestured around to all the clothes scattered about.

"Look, I know that all of this skepticism is driven by your love and concern for me, but on this issue, I need for you to trust me. Yes, I am lonely, Amanda. This house has never been so empty, and this bed has never been so cold. I'm not saying that I want to share my bed with anyone. I know that I am not ready for that. But I am ready for the company of a man." Rozalla picked up the picture of her and Vince off of her nightstand. "No one can ever replace Vince or make me forget about him, but I know that even he wouldn't want me to be lonely and alone."

"What makes you think that he'd be in favor of your dating so soon?"

"If you're so sure that I'm rushing into this, then please tell me what is the appropriate time frame? Two years…five…ten? Should I just allow myself to shrivel up and die alone? I mean really, is Heather going to be the only one on my side with this decision?"

"Is Heather the one that talked you into it?"

"What am I, twelve? I don't need someone to talk me into anything or make my decisions for me. I mean, she may have given me a little nudge. You know, encouraged me not to continue to go day after day without interacting with others. I mean, what am I supposed to do? The girls hardly come around; they don't even call as much as they used to." Rozalla's eyes began to puddle and tears spilled over the rim of her eyes. "Please Amanda, just trust that I know what I'm doing."

"Okay, if this is what you want, then you have my support," Amanda conceded. "But you can't go out like that. Go fix your face while I pull together a couple of outfits for you to choose from."

"Thank you."

Rozalla smiled as she grabbed her makeup bag and went to her bathroom vanity. As she cleansed and applied foundation to her already flawless skin, Amanda sorted through the clothes she had tossed all over the bed. By the time that Rozalla was finished with her hair and makeup, Amanda had hung all of her clothes up except for the beautiful, black and white wrap dress and red pumps she'd chosen for her friend to wear. It wasn't long after Rozalla finished dressing that the doorbell rang.

Amanda looked at her watch to see that it was 7:58 pm. "He's a prompt little bugger, isn't he?"

"How do I look?" Rozalla asked as she nervously smoothed the imaginary wrinkles out of her dress.

"You look beautiful, now go let the man in before he turns around and leaves."

Amanda was hot on her heels as Rozalla made her way to the door. She took one more deep breath before opening the door with a big smile plastered on her face. "Good evening, Corbin, please come in."

"Good evening to you. Wow, you look gorgeous, more beautiful than I remember."

"Thank you. You don't look so bad yourself," she flirted.

"Corbin, I'd like you to meet my dear friend, Amanda. Amanda, this is Corbin."

"Nice to meet you, Amanda." Corbin extended his hand.

Taking his hand in hers, Amanda gave him a firm hand shake. "It's nice to meet you too. I hope you plan to take very good care of my girl tonight. And by take care, I mean be a gentleman, be kind and treat her with respect."

"Of course. My parents raised me right and taught me how to properly treat a lady. I promise you, she's in good hands."

"Well, that's good to know. I'm going to leave now, but you should also know that on my way out, I'm taking a picture of your car as well as your tag number. In fact, I think I'll use my phone to take a picture of you as well."

"Amanda!" Rozalla had a look of complete horror on her face.

"It's okay, Rozalla. I like that your girl is looking out for you." He instantly struck a pose for his close-up.

She snapped his picture, smiled and said, "Thanks, I've got all I need." She'd decided to be open-minded and supportive of her friend's decision to start dating, but this guy left a bad taste in her mouth. There was just something about him that didn't sit well with Amanda. Yeah, he looked good as hell, but looks alone did not make the man, and this man was definitely missing something.

"Good night and Roz, please call me when you're in for the night."

"Okay, I will," Rozalla replied in an almost inaudible voice.

Amanda walked out and just as she'd promised, she lifted her phone and proceeded to take pictures of Corbin's car and tag. She even went so far as to write down an estimate of his height and weight. She didn't actually think she'd have a need for all of it, but better safe than sorry.

CHAPTER SIX

As she walked down the hall to retrieve her purse, Corbin walked around the family room looking at all of Rozalla's family photos. There was her and Vince's wedding photo along with pictures of the girls lining the fireplace mantle. Family vacation photos sat on the end table, more pictures of Rozalla and Vince in the entertainment center, and even their wedding album adorned the coffee table.

"Are you ready to go?" Rozalla asked as she walked up behind Corbin.

"Do you mind if I ask you a question?"

"Not at all. What's on your mind?"

"How long were you two married?"

"We were married for twenty-three years. I was so young and innocent back then," Rozalla replied with a bashful grin.

"You look like a baby in your wedding picture. Exactly how old were you, if you don't mind my asking?"

"I was nineteen and he was my first love."

"Wow, it's a lot to take in. Could be intimidating to a lesser man."

"Why would you, or should I say a lesser man, find any of this intimidating?"

"A guy walks into your home, and sees nothing but evidence of a life of love with what I'd assume was the greatest guy to ever breathe. At least he was in your eyes. Am I wrong?"

"No, you are correct for the most part. However, I learned a long time ago that no one is perfect and as good as it was, our marriage was not without its fair share of bumps in the road. That's what I'm coming to grips with now. The good, bad and indifferent that we shared is no more. I can only hope that one day I'll get a second chance at love. You know, that love of a lifetime."

"You mean to tell me that you spent twenty-three years with someone and he wasn't the love of a lifetime? That sounds like a phenomenal waste of your time."

"Not at all, we had a lot of good times. Not to mention the two beautiful daughters that we created. He was a good man and I would never have wished him dead," she lied. "But now, I have an opportunity to start over. Experience some of the things I never had a chance to in my younger years. I was so busy being a wife and mother that a lot of experiences slipped right by me."

"So am I the first guy you've gone out with since your husband's passing?"

"Yes you are. You are also full of questions," she giggled.

"I'm sorry, I just like to get a feel for what I'm walking into. And it seems like this will be a new experience for me as well."

"How so? You'll never make me believe for two seconds that you've never dated before."

"Oh, I've dated plenty, but I've never dated an older woman." Corbin grinned as if he were the cat that ate the canary.

"Wait, just how old are you?" Rozalla asked with a bit of panic in her voice.

"Calm down there, young lady. I'm only a couple of years younger. I'm thirty-four."

Rozalla plopped down on the couch in disbelief. "Oh my goodness, I'm robbing the cradle! I'm sorry Corbin, I had no idea you were so young. I never would've wasted your time had I known."

"So are you saying that you're not going out with me now?"

"I can't. You are far too young for me, honey. But you still have time to catch up with your boys, have some drinks, and whistle at all the young girls in the bar."

"You can't be serious! If I'd wanted to date some young girl, I would've gone to a college campus and found one. I want to date you. You're sexy, beautiful, and clearly we can hold a good conversation. So why don't you forget about the age difference and let's go enjoy a good meal, take in some sights, and see how it goes?"

Rozalla hesitantly agreed, all the while hoping that she wasn't making a huge mistake. Three hours later, they had enjoyed a great meal at J Alexander's and were walking hand in hand towards the Sky View Ferris wheel near Centennial Olympic Park. The closer they got to the gigantic wheel, the more afraid Rozalla became. Vince had tried to get her to ride it with him when it first came to Atlanta, but her fear wouldn't allow her to do so. Now here she was with this fine, handsome, young man and she didn't want to disappoint him. However, her fear was still very strong.

"Are you okay, beautiful? You've gotten awfully quiet on me."

"I've gotta tell you, that contraption scares the hell out of me. It's so freaking big and you're so high up. I'm sorry, but I don't think I can ride that."

"Come on, Rozalla, you said yourself that this is your opportunity to experience new things. Besides, I'll be holding your hand the entire time," Corbin reassured her as he playfully rubbed his shoulder against hers. "C'mon sexy, I promise it'll be okay."

"Okay, let's do it," she said as she found her courage.

The hardest part of the ride was the decision to step in the bucket, but Rozalla was so glad she did. The view of the city from that high up was amazing. There seemed to be a million stars in the sky and even the air she breathed seemed cleaner. The fact that Corbin was stroking her hair and whispering sweet nothings in her ear didn't hurt at all. When the ride was over, they took the scenic route and walked hand in hand through the park, and on to the car. Soft jazz accompanied them on the ride back to Rozalla's house and every note of it seemed perfect.

"Thank you, I really enjoyed myself."

Watching her unlock the door, Corbin whispered, "It doesn't have to end."

"Unfortunately it does. I have to be up and out really early tomorrow."

"I promise to let you sleep. I'll lay beside you, quiet as a church mouse."

The thought of a warm body lying beside her was very appealing, but she knew that she wasn't quite ready for what would come with the cuddling. "Tempting, but I don't think that I'm ready to take that step yet. You understand, right?"

"Of course. How about we make plans for mid-week?"

"Thursday is the end of my work week. Will that work for you?"

"Absolutely, you can come over to my house and I'll cook dinner for you."

Rozalla smiled broadly, "That sounds like a great plan. Thanks again and enjoy the rest of your night."

Corbin wrapped her in a warm embrace and kissed her on the cheek. "Thanks and you do the same." As she closed the door, he turned and headed home.

The house was so quiet, but tonight it just didn't seem quite as lonely. Rozalla kicked off her shoes, grabbed a bottle of water from the refrigerator, and headed to her bedroom. As she stripped off her clothes, she remembered that she hadn't checked her phone for messages in a couple of days. There was a call from a telemarketer and surprisingly, a message from Lisa. She said she'd drop by for a bit tomorrow evening and Rozalla hoped that it would be a pleasant meeting. Her last message was from Amanda. Beep—"Hey girl, call me as soon as you get in. If I don't hear from you by 1am I'm calling the cops." Rozalla laughed and decided to go take a shower before calling Amanda back.

"Hello."

"Hey, did I wake you up?"

"That must've been a hell of a date, because you sound happy as hell."

"I must admit, it was a great date. We went to dinner. Girl, have you ever had the carrot cake at J Alexander's? That is the best, moistest cake I've ever had in my life," Rozalla proclaimed. "But anyway, after dinner we went downtown and rode that giant Ferris wheel. We ended the night with a nice walk through the park. He was a complete gentleman."

"I'm glad you enjoyed yourself, but I can't believe you rode that Ferris wheel. Didn't Vince try to get you to ride that with him?"

"Yes he did, but I was too scared back then. I've decided to step out of my shell, to start taking a few more chances in life."

"I see… So do you plan to see him again?"

"Yes indeed, he's cooking me dinner Thursday after work. And before you can ask, no… I didn't kiss him. He gave me a kiss on the cheek and we said goodnight."

"All right now Ms. Thang, I'm glad you enjoyed yourself. But it's past my bedtime and now that I know you made it home safely, I'll be able to sleep like a rock."

"Wait, before you go, why don't you come over for dinner tomorrow? Lisa is coming over and I figured I'd see if I could get Carmen to come up too. It's been a long time since I cooked fish and pasta. That was Vince's favorite Saturday dinner and the girls loved it as well."

"Sure, count me in. I'll see you tomorrow, girl. Goodnight."

CHAPTER SEVEN

There must have been five pounds of tilapia on the kitchen counter. Each piece patiently waited for its turn in the baptismal pool of canola oil. While the fish waited, Rozalla stirred her large pot of linguine with garlic sauce and shrimp. She always liked to cook it first, so that the pasta and shrimp could sit and soak up all the flavor of the sauce. She heard the door slam and guessed that it was Lisa arriving. She was the only one that never learned to close a door without almost knocking it off the hinges.

"Come on back, I'm in the kitchen."

"Mama, you didn't even know who was walking up in here. I could've been a serial killer and you'd have invited me back to kill you," Lisa fussed as she always did.

"Hello to you too, darling. How about you come give me a hug and keep all that nagging. Besides, a serial killer wouldn't have had a key for that locked door."

Lisa walked over to her mom, and despite the anger she was still harboring towards Rozalla, she wrapped her arms around her and planted a light kiss on her cheek. Her mom smiled and kissed her back. Although she knew her mom would object, Lisa grabbed a fork out of the drawer and dug a heap of pasta out of the pot.

"Girl, if you don't stop eating out of my pot, I'm going to hurt you!"

"But Mom, it's been so long since I've had this and oh goodness, it tastes so good."

"As hard as I've been in here slaving, it had better be good. Now put the fork down and wait until dinner is served."

"Fine, but can you please tell me why you're cooking so much? Two pieces of fish is typically my limit, but there's enough food here to feed a small army."

Rozalla looked at Lisa and rolled her eyes. "Since when have you stopped at just two pieces? The last time I cooked this meal, you ate double that. Your dad was convinced that you were going to grow fins."

"Okay, so I like fish, but you still haven't answered my question."

"Well, Amanda is on her way over, and I even convinced your sister to come up from Athens and join us for dinner. I think she may actually spend the night with me. You know, we'd love to have you join our little slumber party."

"Humph, I'll think about it."

"Stop trying to play hard, girl. You know you want to stay. Remember how the three of us would sit up late night watching movies, eating popcorn and talking about the little knotty head boys y'all were crushing on?"

"Of course I do," Lisa smiled. "And Daddy would serenade us with his loud snoring. He'd get so loud that we'd have to blast the TV just to drown him out."

"I used to tell him all the time that all that snoring wasn't healthy and he'd always say, 'Woman, that just means I'm in the zone,' remember?"

"Remember what?" Carmen asked as she entered the kitchen.

"Hey baby, I didn't hear you come in," Rozalla chirped as she wiped her hands on her apron, and gave her oldest daughter a big hug. We were talking about how loudly your dad used to snore."

"Oh my goodness, he used to sound like a freaking buzz saw. Hey sis, how long have you been here?"

"Just long enough for Mama to talk me into joining you all for a little slumber party." Lisa rolled her eyes in mock annoyance.

"Girl, you are so fake. You know you want to spend the night with us. You probably already have an overnight bag in the car, just in case we asked you to stay. Am I right?"

"Whatever, Carmen, you make me sick, always thinking you know me. I just happen to keep a tote bag full of clothes and toiletries in case of an accident," she lied, and they all burst into laughter.

The three of them quickly fell into their old routine with Rozalla cooking, Carmen making fresh-squeezed lemonade, and Lisa setting the kitchen table. Rozalla looked around at the girls and it all felt so normal, so comfortable. She loved Vince, but with the three of them there, she wasn't missing him. Of course she thought of him often, but with the passing of each day, she was looking forward to starting a new life without him more and more. Sure, he was a good guy, but no one was perfect; he had his faults just like everyone else. Yes, it was sad that he was gone at such a young age, but this was her opportunity to start living the life she missed out on by marrying so young. She wasn't exactly sure what she'd missed, but she was looking forward to finding out. Her only concern was getting the girls to accept that she deserved a chance to start over and experience a fulfilled life. But she would worry about all that later, for now, she would be grateful for this time with her daughters. She'd be glad that they were seemingly moving past the ill feelings that her poor behavior had left them with.

Just as she dropped the last three pieces of fish in the oil, the doorbell rang. "Would one of you please let Amanda in?"

"I got it," Lisa sang as she placed the last fork on the table and bolted for the front door. "Hi Ms. Amanda, come on in. How are you today?"

Amanda reached and gave Lisa a big hug. "I'm doing great, sweetie, how are you?"

"I'm fine. Come on back, we're in the kitchen getting ready for this great meal Mama has cooked."

"It smells good. As crazy as it sounds, I love the smell of fish."

"Really?" Lisa asked with a turned up nose.

"Girl, don't look at me like that. You know what I mean, fresh-cooked fish. Not stinky, funky fish," Amanda clarified.

"Okay, whatever you say, Ms. Amanda."

"Hi ladies. You've got it smelling good in here, Roz, and I swear I'm as hungry as a hostage."

"Hey girl, I'm taking the last piece of fish out now."

"Hey Ms. Amanda, how are you?" Carmen greeted her with a warm hug.

"Hi Carmen, how's business going?"

"It's great actually." As they all sat for dinner, Carmen continued on with her unexpected good news. "I hadn't had a chance to tell y'all, but I got approached yesterday by another salon owner. She caters primarily to Caucasian customers, and since my customers are majority African American, she thought we should discuss opening a salon together. By bringing our talents together and crossing demographics, we could have the biggest and most successful salon in the Athens area. Wouldn't that be great?"

"Oh baby, that is a great idea, but would you close your salon on campus? It's such a thriving business," Rozalla asked with concern in her voice.

"No, we'd both keep our existing salons and either rent or purchase a new space near the Georgia Square Mall. Of course, we'd have to hire a few new stylists, but I could see this being a very profitable venture."

"I think it's a brilliant idea," Lisa beamed with excitement. "You already have the market cornered at the university and now you could have an even bigger piece of the pie. Next thing we know, you'll be expanding into a chain of salons across the country."

Carmen burst out laughing, "Slow down a little bit, sis. We're gonna see how this expansion works out first."

"Wow, Carmen, your dad would be so proud of you. This really is a great opportunity and I know you'll make it a huge success," Amanda added with sincerity in her voice.

"I couldn't be more proud if I tried. An entrepreneur and a nurse, I really lucked out in the kid department. Amanda's right, your dad would be proud of both of you. Now how about we hold hands and pray over this meal?"

Rozalla thanked God for the food, family, friends and fellowship. The foursome ate and talked as if they hadn't been together in five years. Lisa told them about the new guy she was dating and how she was enjoying being on her own for the first time. Carmen talked about the bump in the road she and her longtime boyfriend had hit, but were thankfully moving past. Amanda, well as oddly attractive as she was, she still hadn't found anyone that she deemed worthy. Amanda wasn't what many considered a classic beauty. She was slim with an athletic build and a nose that resembled a bird's beak, narrow and pointy. However, her smooth skin, gorgeous smile, and beautiful personality made her a real knock-out. Rozalla felt that the only reason she hadn't been able to snag Mr. Right was because she was far too picky.

"So what about you, Mama, when do you think you'll be ready to dip your toe back into the dating pool?" Carmen asked. The surprised look on everyone's face let her know that no one expected that question. Rozalla and Amanda just glanced at each other, too scared to let their look linger for fear the girls might suspect something. The scowl on her face let them all know that Lisa was very unpleasantly surprised.

"Why would you ask that, Carmen? Daddy's only been gone for six months. She hasn't even had time to properly mourn his loss yet."

"Dang Lisa, I'm sorry. You don't have to get so upset about it. I didn't really expect her to answer. I know it's only been a few months and no, I don't think she's ready now, but you'll have to eventually get used to the idea of Mama dating."

"You two are really getting caught up in a pointless conversation. Trust me, I won't date before I'm really ready and clearly I'm not ready yet," Rozalla lied.

Amanda looked at her with confusion. She couldn't understand why Rozalla wouldn't say something to try and prep the girls for the possibility of dating soon, instead of flat out lying to their faces. So she decided to try and prep them her damn self.

"You say you're not ready, Rozalla, but you never know. I know what it's like to be lonely, and I certainly wouldn't wish it on you. And they say that people who've been in a long- term marriage often have to take a mate sooner than most."

"And why is that, Ms. Amanda?" Lisa asked with attitude.
"Because the sudden loneliness starts to negatively affect their health. Why do you think that older couples who've been together for decades often die only months apart?"

"Well, Mama isn't one of those older people. She's still a young woman and can take as much time as she needs to heal," Lisa was adamant.

Rozalla was desperate for this conversation to end. Lisa was becoming more upset by the minute. She couldn't really gauge how Carmen would truly feel about her dating and didn't care to find out right now. When the doorbell rang, she breathed a huge sigh of relief. Grateful for the interruption, Rozalla jumped up from the table and darted off to the front door. And to her surprise, Heather was standing there with a bottle of wine in hand, ready for some girl talk. Heather followed her friend into the kitchen and her presence sent everyone else's attitude from bad to worse.

"Hi everybody," Heather chirped in her annoying little perky voice. "I didn't realize you guys were having a girl's night. I hope my dropping by isn't too much of an intrusion?"

Holding onto her manners, Carmen answered her through clenched teeth. "Of course not, come on in."

Heather didn't hesitate to plop down in a chair. "Ooh, is there an extra plate?" She didn't wait for food to be offered, and when Rozalla gave her a plate, she piled the fish on and began to chow down, smacking her lips and all.

"So, did your mom tell you the good news?" Heather asked as she licked her fingers. "She had a hot date last night and I'm here to hear all the details!"

CHAPTER EIGHT

The fallout from Heather's little outburst was far worse than Rozalla could've ever imagined. The room fell so quiet that you could hear a mouse piss on a carpet. Unfortunately, it didn't last very long. Lisa jumped to her feet like she was ready to do battle.

"Ms. Amanda, did you know about this date?"

"Take a seat Lisa and we'll all talk it out," Amanda pled.

"No ma'am, I won't be sitting. I just want to know if you knew about this date and if you encouraged it?"

"I found out about the date earlier yesterday. Once it was brought to light and I was unable to get your mother to reconsider, I came over and helped her prepare for it."

"Lisa, sit down," Carmen encouraged as she tugged at her baby sister's arm.

Snatching her arm from Carmen's grip, Lisa began to spit venom at the two remaining women. "So, let me see if I've got this right. You talked my poor, grieving mother into going out on a date with some stranger and she was ignorant, or desperate enough to do it. Which is it, Mama, were you stupid, desperate, or do you just not give a damn about Daddy and the fact that he just died? I mean, damn, do you really think that six months is a respectable amount of time to mourn the man that dedicated his life to you? Or are you so much of a slut that you can't wait to get back out there and get laid? Is that funky, old twat of yours that hungry for attention?"

"What the hell is wrong with you, Lisa? How dare you talk to Mama like that, you disrespectful little brat," Carmen hissed.

"Little girl, you have no idea what I've been through, what I'm still going through. And for you to talk to me, your mother, like that… Get out!" Rozalla pushed herself up from her seat. "Get out of my house, Lisa, now!" Rozalla pushed her daughter's shoulders with more force than she realized she had. "Get out now, you hear me? Get out!"

Despite Lisa's objections and rants about the house belonging to her father, Rozalla continued to yell and physically push her out backwards until Lisa's back was against the front door.

"You think your daddy was the only one that dedicated himself to this marriage, to this family? What do you think I was doing all those years? Who cooked and cleaned behind you kids and your father? Who listened to him at night as he talked about all the stresses of his day? Who comforted him when his parents died? Who solely supported this family financially after the accident that rendered him disabled for nine months? Who stayed up late nights helping with homework and tending to the sick? It was me, Lisa, me! And don't forget that it's been my paycheck paying your tuition. Now it's my turn to live, without having the responsibility of all y'all on my damn back. And until you are ready to apologize, realize I'm a grown ass woman, and treat me with the respect that I deserve, don't come back to *my* house."

"Screw you and your house," Lisa spat as she stormed out the door. Rozalla turned around to see three stunned faces staring back at her.

"I love you so much, Mama, but I never realized that your loving and supporting us was such an uncomfortable weight on your back. I promise that I will not impose my weight upon you any longer," Carmen sniffed as she picked up her bags and left.

"Wait a minute, Carmen, I didn't mean it like that. Please don't leave, I didn't mean it like that," Rozalla begged, but her pleas fell on deaf ears. Carmen pulled off without looking back.

Rozalla closed the door and slid down to the floor. Her hands covered her eyes as she sobbed like a baby. She wondered what she'd done so wrong that would make Lisa treat her with such disrespect. Furthermore, how could she in turn make her kids feel as if they'd been an unwanted responsibility? She was hurt and angry at the entire situation, but still felt deep down that this was her time to live. Was that really so wrong?

"Come on, Roz, get up and let's go back into the kitchen. I'll fix some coffee and we can talk it all out," Amanda said as she helped her best friend to her feet.

As Rozalla sat at the table trying to collect herself, she thought of all that had just transpired and wondered how it all could've been avoided.

"Amanda, why did you have to say that you tried to convince me not to go through with the date? Why couldn't you just defend me and my choice to go out?"

"That's what I was wondering," added Heather.

Amanda looked at Heather as if she wanted to knock her out of her chair. Pointing at her, Amanda commented, "You don't want to start with me." She then turned her attention to Rozalla. "Don't you think the bigger question is why did this chick announce your date to everyone in the first place?"

"How was she supposed to know that Lisa would overreact?"

"Isn't she supposed to be your friend? I assumed that y'all would have talked about how your daughters might feel about the whole dating thing. And then there's the common sense factor. Wouldn't common sense tell her to clear that conversation with you first?"

"Wait a damn minute," Heather interjected. "I know you're not calling me stupid."

"I didn't, but if the shoe fits, feel free to put it on your big foot."

"You better watch your mouth before this big foot finds it way up your tight ass."

"Shut up! Both of you please shut the hell up," Rozalla demanded. "Amanda, you're right; I should've had that conversation with Heather, but I didn't. But you, you knew all along what a mess this could turn into. And instead of avoiding it, you sat there and lit the match that set off the explosion. I expected more from you. I expected for my best friend to be on my side and help me explain things to my daughters in an appropriate way. I can't believe you, it's like you wanted all this mess to happen."

"You can't be serious. This tramp blurts out your business and you blame me? You need to realize that I'm the best friend and confidant you've got. Unjustly accusing me and creating this distance between you and the girls is not something you want to do, Rozalla. You need to think long and hard about what you're doing."

Heather popped out of her seat and right into Amanda's face. "Call me out of my name one more time and— "

"And what? Tramp you'd better sit down out of my face before I knock you down."

"Enough of this! Amanda, it's time for you to leave. It's clear that you're not in my corner when it comes to how I want to move on with my life. Since you can't support it, well, maybe it's time that you removed yourself from it," Rozalla offered.

"I can't believe you. We've been friends for thirty years and this is how you treat me?" Amanda said with disbelief. "Fine, enjoy your new life and this trick that you think is your friend." She grabbed her things and left with tears in her eyes.

Rozalla dropped back down to the kitchen table with her head in her hands. How did this wonderful evening of family and fellowship go so wrong? She didn't think she'd ever understand why her girls, or her so-called friend, didn't want to see her living a happy and fulfilled life. Thank God for Heather, she understood Rozalla's loneliness and encouraged her in her pursuit of a new, happy life.

"Forget them, Rozalla. I know you love them, but this is your time. Your husband is gone, your kids are grown, and this is your time to start life anew. Girl, it's time to turn up!"

Rozalla couldn't help but to giggle. "You are so silly, but very accurate. This is my time!"

CHAPTER NINE

It seemed as if the week was dragging to Rozalla. Maybe because she could hardly wait for her Thursday night dinner date. She'd talked to Corbin every day since their first date. Some of their conversations seemed to have gone on for hours. Rozalla felt giddy about their talks and the idea of being pursued again. Maybe it was her sheer anticipation that made the days seem so long. Either way, she was happy and excited to have something to look forward to. The phone rang, pulling Rozalla from her thoughts. She sighed as she reached to the other side of her sleigh bed and grabbed her cell phone from the night table.

"Hey Heather, what's up?"

"Tomorrow night is your big date night, girl."

"You don't have to remind me, I haven't been able to think of anything else. I've been racking my brain over what to wear, what kind of wine I should take with me, if I should let him kiss me or not. As you can see, my mind is flying."

"I see! Rozalla, you're going to have to calm down and just relax with it. I know that the dating thing is new to you, but I promise it's better if you're not so uptight and worried about every detail. Throw on some jeans, a nice blouse, and some heels. Take a nice Moscato and if he kisses you, enjoy it."

"Wow, you make it sound so easy."

"It is easy. Have you heard from either of your girls?"

"No, I don't expect to hear from them for quite some time. Lisa is pissed and Carmen is hurt. I know you didn't know any better, but I sure wish you had held your question until we were alone."

"You know I'm sorry, Rozalla, I never meant to cause any problems between you and your daughters. But let's not forget, Amanda is the real problem here. All she had to do was back you up. Instead, she threw you all up under the bus."

"I know, but I shouldn't have been surprised, Amanda is honest if nothing else. I'm sure she meant no harm, but she should've found a way to be truthful without making me look so bad."

"Well, now you know who your real friend is," Heather snorted.

Rozalla thought for a moment about what a true friend Amanda had been throughout the years, but decided to not discuss the situation any further. "Anyway, I'm about to roll over and go to sleep. I'll chat with you tomorrow.

"All right, call me as soon as you get in from your date."

"Will do. Goodnight."

After disconnecting with Heather, all Rozalla really wanted to do was call Amanda. She was so accustomed to sharing everything with her and this disconnect between them felt very strange, very uncomfortable. But again, it was Amanda that chose to turn against her when all she wanted was to find a little happiness.

~~~

She stood nervously on Corbin's front porch and took several deep breaths. Rozalla was trying to calm her nerves and desperately trying to talk herself out of turning and running back home. Yes, this was her time, but was she really ready to be with someone in such an intimate setting. She hadn't gone to a man's home for dinner and drinks since she'd dated Vince. It was different then, it was a more innocent time, they were young and the nervousness that overwhelmed her now was non-existent back then.

"Do you plan to stand out there all night?" Corbin asked as he cracked the door.

"Oh, I didn't realize that you'd heard me out here. But look, I came bearing gifts," Rozalla smiled as she lifted the bottle in his direction.

"Nothing like a good bottle of wine. Why don't you come on in and let's crack it open?"

Corbin stepped back and opened the door wide, allowing Rozalla room to enter. She crossed the threshold and waited for her date to lead the way. Once he'd locked the door, Corbin took her by the hand and led her through the foyer, past the family room, and into the kitchen. Along the way, Rozalla took in all the details of his home and noted how well and tastefully decorated it was, especially for a single man. Although she did think it odd that he didn't have one single picture of himself or his family on display.

"Your home is beautiful, did you decorate it yourself?"

"I actually hired an interior designer. She did a great job and while I love it, I think it needs a good dose of masculinity. She's been showing me a few pieces that I'm considering swapping some of this stuff out for."

"I agree with the fact that she did a great job. It's all quite lovely," Rozalla complimented as she continued to take in her surroundings. "Mind if I ask you a question?"

"I'm an open book, ask me anything."

"I haven't seen one picture of you or your family. Is there a reason that you don't like to display photos?"

"I was raised by a single mother until her untimely death. I was only eight when she passed and I didn't have any other family that was interested in taking me in. So I spent the next ten years as a ward of the state. And I think that having a bunch of pictures of myself is a little vain," he replied with a crooked smile.

"I'm so sorry." Rozalla had sympathy written all over her face. "That sounds like a very lonely childhood. But look at you now, a successful attorney. You certainly took your lemons and made a sweet lemonade."

"Thank you. I worked hard and have thankfully made a comfortable life for myself. Now all I have to do is find a good woman to share it with," he said with a wink. "Now how about that wine?" Corbin lifted a beautiful goblet and passed it to Rozalla.

"Shall we make a toast?"

"Of course. Here's to you, Rozalla and to the wonderful opportunity we've been given to get to know one another."

They drank and enjoyed good conversation as Corbin put the finishing touches on dinner. Rozalla was still struck by his taste in décor, cookware, and even the fine china that he set the table with. Everything was beautiful, he was so intelligent and the atmosphere was charged with the physical attraction they had for one another. Rozalla knew that she was getting caught up in it all a little too quickly. She needed a minute to clear her head.

"May I please use your restroom to freshen up?"

"Of course, it's right down the hall to the left." Corbin watched as Rozalla sashayed down the hall. Looking at her shapely body in those jeans had him licking his lips.

Rozalla took a long look at herself in the mirror and wondered if she was really ready for what the rest of the night might hold. Was she ready to have this man kissing on her and putting thoughts of intimacy in her head? While her mind told her to proceed with caution, her body screamed *I'm ready*! She washed her hands and was touching up her lipstick when she heard screaming.

"What the hell is going on here, Corbin? I thought you were working late," the female voice shouted.

"Baby, let me explain--"

"Explain what? Why there's some other woman's lipstick on my damn wine glass, why the table is set for two, or why you're in here cooking like Chef Boyardee?"

"Corbin, I can't believe you. I know I raised you better than this," another woman's voice echoed.

Rozalla began to panic as she listened from the bathroom. Her mind swirled as she contemplated how she could retrieve her purse and get the hell out of there.

"Where is she, Corbin? The heifer's purse is here so where is she hiding? She's bad-ass enough to sit up in my home like she belongs here, so she needs to be bad-ass enough to show her face. Where are you, bitch?" The first voice called out.

Rozalla took a deep breath and began the fearful walk down the hall. Once she stepped into the family room, all eyes were on her.

"How dare you come into my home! Who the hell are you?"

"Please accept my apology, I had no idea that this was your home." Rozalla's fear began to change to anger. "Corbin told me that he was single. When I asked about the lack of family photos, he told me that his mother died and he grew up as a ward of the state. Therefore there were no pictures."

"You told her that I died?" The older woman asked.

"Mom, she must have misunderstood. And Rhonda, baby, I just had a moment of weakness, but I swear I didn't touch her. Baby you've got to forgive me, please."

Rozalla was floored. How could she have been so fooled by him? Corbin was a lying, weak excuse of a man. "This is unfreaking believable." She moved towards the counter to get her purse and leave, but this Rhonda chick snatched it up. Rozalla rolled her eyes in disgust. "May I please have my bag?"

"You'll get it when I'm ready to give it to you. Have you slept with my husband?"

"No, this is only my second time seeing him, and as I said, he told me he was single. Now give me my bag."

"When was the first time you saw him?"

"I met him last week at a bar, now give me my bag," Rozalla's annoyance was evident in her voice.

Rhonda tossed the purse on the floor. "There's your bag, you raggedy tramp. Now get the hell out of my house."

"Gladly, you dumb ass," Rozalla shot back as she snatched up her purse and left. She jumped in her car and sped away. As she made her way home, she replayed what had just happened over and over in her head. Is this what she had to look forward to? Was the dating pool going to be filled with lying, sneaking, cheating, and conniving men?

Her mind flashed back to when she went over to Vince's home for the first time. He was such a gentleman. He ordered take out and they ate it on his floor in front of the television. They talked openly and honestly about their lives. Both shared what they had experienced and what they wanted out of life. She knew that she could trust every word he said, she could believe in the promises he made. Were there no more men like that? Was the foolishness she'd just experienced going to be the norm? If so, she no longer had any interest what-so-ever in dating. Rozalla walked in her house, stripped off her clothes, and jumped into a hot shower. Falling across her bed, she grabbled Vince's old pillow and cried herself to sleep.

CHAPTER TEN

The phone had been ringing incessantly for the last two days. If it wasn't that lying Corbin, it was Heather. Rozalla had no intention of ever answering Corbin's calls and for now, she didn't want to speak to Heather either. Maybe everyone else had been right, it was too soon for her to be dating. The phone rang again and the caller id revealed that once again, it was Corbin. And once again, Rozalla hit the decline button. She shoved the phone back in her pocket, got her belongings out of her locker at work, and headed for the parking lot. Just as she unlocked her car door, she heard someone yelling her name.

"Rozalla wait," Heather called as she sprinted towards the car. When she finally reached Rozalla, she bent over panting, trying to catch her breath. She raised up and threw her blonde locks over her shoulders. "Why haven't you returned any of my calls?"

"I've been pulling extra shifts this week and I've been really tired," Rozalla lied.

"Um no, try again. I checked your schedule and I know that you haven't worked a single minute over your normal time. Now what's really going on? I've been dying to know how your date went the other night."

"Haven't I told you about checking my schedule?"

"What's wrong with you? You're dodging me like I'm a freaking bill collector or something, lying to me, and you've got a snotty attitude to boot. If I've done something, you need to have balls enough to tell me."

Rozalla looked at her friend and remembered why she didn't like working at the same facility with the women she hung out with. There was no escaping the heifers. But then she shook her head and realized that Heather really was in the dark about everything that had transpired. Treating her coldly was not fair.

"Look, the other night was an absolute mess. I was dodging the calls just to give myself a minute to clear my head and see if this dating thing is really right for me right now."

"I get off in a couple of hours. Why don't you meet me at Tin Lizzy's for a drink and a cheap meal? That'll give you time to get home, change and then we can talk it all out."

Rozalla reluctantly agreed and then headed home to relax for a bit before heading back out. As she maneuvered through the streets, she had to fight the urge to call Amanda. She wasn't ready to hear all of the *I told you so's* that would surely be thrown her way. But at the same time, it felt so unnatural not to share all of this with her friend. Tears formed in the corners of Rozalla's eyes. She'd not only lost Vince, but her best friend and her daughters had turned away from her. Maybe it wasn't the right time to start dating, but they should've remained supportive and allowed her to find out just as she had, the hard way.

Her thirty-minute power nap wasn't nearly enough, but Rozalla got up anyway and headed out the door. A short ride led her to the entrance of Tin Lizzy's. There were only a few tables that were occupied, so she was able to get her favorite little corner table. Rozalla loved this little Mexican cantina for the fried jalapeños that they served and the margaritas weren't bad either. She ordered her drink and scrolled through her Facebook page on her phone while she waited for Heather to arrive.

"Do you always eat alone?"

"Excuse me?" Rozalla replied as she looked up into the face of a somewhat handsome man. He was tall with a thick build that cast a shadow over her screen.

"I just noticed that you were here alone. Most women are too insecure to go out and eat alone. Your confidence is very appealing and I thought I'd see if maybe you wanted a dinner companion?"

"No offense, but I'm not interested in your company. Thank you and goodbye."

"Bitch," the stranger mumbled as he turned and walked away, almost bumping into Heather.

"Excuse you, you rude jackass!" Rozalla barked a little too loudly.

"What is all that about?" Heather asked as she pulled a chair out and took a seat in front of Rozalla.

"This is why I can't be bothered trying to date. Men are either rude with no home training, liars, cheaters or just plain old worthless. He's mad because I didn't want his company. What kind of man calls a woman out of her name just because she's not interested?"

"Girl, I'm going to need you to take a sip of your drink and calm down. You can't let one trifling man ruin it for all of them."

Heather waived down the waitress and ordered a pitcher of margaritas, fried jalapeños and nachos. Looking across the table at Rozalla, she could see distress written all over her face. She'd actually grown afraid as she wondered what had happened to her friend on that date. Had Rozalla been raped, had he robbed her, threatened her?

"Okay, I can't take it anymore. What in the world did he do to you? What happened the other night?"

As Rozalla recounted the events of the other night, she was shocked by Heather's lack of concern. She couldn't understand why her so-called friend looked as if everything that had transpired was no big deal. Even when she told her about Corbin's wife tossing her purse to the floor, she didn't react.

"Do you understand what I'm telling you? It was horrible."

"I hear you, Rozalla and all I have to say is welcome to the dating game. All things considered, it wasn't nearly as bad as it could've been."

"Well damn, how much worse can it get? You know what, never mind, I don't even want to know."

Heather leaned back in her seat, sighing deeply. "I know that you're used to being taken care of and I know that you were courted by Vince back in the day. But you need to realize that times have changed. Do you realize that in Atlanta there are like ten women for every man? The competition is stiff and the men know that they can get away with damn near anything, because the women are desperate. And we won't even speak of the men that have traded teams."

"Traded teams?"

"Yeah, they've decided that they prefer to be with other men. Have you not looked around and noticed that you're now in the new gay capital?"

"This is all too much for me," Rozalla whimpered as she sucked down the rest of her drink. "All I want is a nice guy, someone from the old school of manners, decency, and chivalry. He doesn't have to look like Denzel or have the body of The Rock. But he does need to be kind, mannerable, respectful, self-sufficient, and attentive.

"Girl, you just described the man that's on every woman's wish list. You need to realize that in order to find your next prince, you're going to have to kiss a few frogs. There are still some good guys out there somewhere. But until you find one, why not enjoy the company and sexual satisfaction of a few toads?"

Heather laughed as though she'd just said the funniest thing ever, but Rozalla failed to see the humor. She knew that Heather was just trying to give her a realistic perspective of today's dating world, but this perspective made her want to go join a convent. At that moment, Rozalla decided that she'd wait a little longer before dipping her toe back in the murky waters of the dating pool. She'd also decided that it was time for her to go. She was mentally drained and wasn't in the right head-space to entertain the foolishness seeping from Heather's mouth.

"All right girlie, I'm out of here," Rozalla said as she dropped twenty-five dollars on the table and stood to leave. "I'll call you a little later."

"Okay."

Heather stood and hugged Rozalla goodbye. Just as Rozalla turned to leave, she bumped into someone, spilling her purse's contents all over the floor. She apologized and instantly stooped down to retrieve her things. She hadn't looked at the stranger until his hand brushed against hers and their eyes met.

"Let me help you with that," the stranger offered.

"I'm so sorry, I should've been watching where I was going."

"I'm glad you weren't. This gave me an opportunity to bask in your beauty for a few moments."

That was probably one of the corniest lines she'd ever heard but still, Rozalla couldn't help but smile. "Thank you for the compliment."

"No thanks necessary, I was only speaking the truth," he replied as he handed her a lipstick case. He looked at her hands and took note of the empty ring finger. "By the way, I'm Harrison."

"Nice name, Harrison. I'm Rozalla and it's nice to meet you. Thanks for helping me get my things and I hope you enjoy the rest of your day."

"Before you leave, may I ask you out to dinner? I promise to be a complete gentleman."

"Harrison, I have no doubt that you're a true gentleman, but I'm recently widowed and don't think that I'm quite ready to step back out there. But thank you for asking."

Disappointment was written all over Harrison's face, but Rozalla didn't let it faze her as she continued her walk out the door. Yes, he was tall, perfectly tanned, with a beautifully chiseled body. Rozalla thought that if she were to ever date a white guy, he'd be it. But her head told her to keep on walking. She was about to ease into her car when she heard someone calling her name. Yep, it was Harrison's fine ass sprinting through the parking lot.

"I know you said that you weren't ready to start dating. I understand and respect that, but may I please give you my number anyway? You know, just in case you ever change your mind."

His smile was so sweet; those perfect white teeth were clearly clouding Rozalla's judgement because she fell for the oldest trick in the book.

"Okay fine, what's your number?"

"Unfortunately, I'm all out of business cards, but here, let me text it to you," he said as he quickly typed out a message. "What number should I text it to?"

Not thinking, Rozalla quickly called out the digits for her cell phone. "Well, I need to be on my way, but if I feel the need for a little conversation, I'll be sure to call you. Goodbye Harrison."

She turned up the volume on the radio and headed home. She was tempted to stop and look around Perimeter Mall, but quickly changed her mind. One of her favorite shows, *So You Think You Can Dance*, was premiering tonight and she didn't want to miss any of it. It's what helped get her though the rough summer months until her all-time favorite, *Scandal*, returned. Thankfully, traffic was much lighter than usual and Rozalla was able to breeze through the city. She was singing along to an oldie but goodie when the phone rang through the car speakers, interrupting her groove.

"Hello?"

"What's up with that gorgeous guy you bumped into? I saw him chasing you down in the parking lot," Heather commented.

"Yeah, that seems to happening a lot today," Rozalla giggled. "He asked me out, but when I said no, he came out and asked if he could give me his number. I figured what's the harm."

"So what's his name and what's on his business card? You know, what does he do for a living?"

"I have no idea. He was out of business cards, so he texted me his number."

Heather started laughing and Rozalla couldn't understand why. She hadn't cracked any jokes. Was it that funny that someone wanted to go out with her?

"What's so freaking funny?"

"Girl, you know you gave him your number, right? You gave him your number so that he could text you," Heather continued to giggle.

"Aww damn, I fell for the okeydokey, didn't I?"

"Yep, you did. But he's fine as hell and hopefully, he'll be respectful and wait for you to call him."

"I certainly hope so. Well honey, I'm home," Rozalla said as she pulled into the garage. "I'll talk to you sometime tomorrow. Bye."

CHAPTER ELEVEN

It had been weeks since Rozalla had done anything outside of work. Heather had tried to convince her to go out again, but Rozalla just kept turning her down. It seemed as if she were still punishing herself for going out on that first date. The loneliness, however, was starting to get to her. She'd called her daughters, but only Carmen had actually answered the phone. Carmen's tone was dry and their conversation was short. It was clear that she wasn't ready to return to the close relationship she'd always had with her mom. Rozalla's next call was to Amanda. She was prepared to apologize for her hurtful comments and offer to take her out to dinner. Yet that was another call that went unanswered.

Rozalla plopped down on the sofa with the television remote. She flipped channels and within two minutes of watching the Bette Midler classic, *Beaches*, she was reduced to a puddle of tears. Her house was so quiet, so empty, and she was so lonely. She dabbed at her eyes and wondered if any of her friends would be there for her the way Bette was for her friend in the movie. She'd always been able to count on Amanda's friendship, but now it looked like all she had left was Heather. No one seemed to understand where Heather was coming from when it came to the things she encouraged Rozalla to do, but Rozalla completely understood and was grateful for the friendship. All Heather wanted was to see her friend living a happy, full life. One full of love, companionship, and a few of the finer luxuries of life. Rozalla wanted those things for herself, but right now they seemed so very far away. As the tears started to flow again, the phone rang, providing a temporary distraction.

"Hello."

"May I please speak with Rozalla?"

"This is she."

"Hi Rozalla, this is Harrison. I know that you said you'd call me when you were ready to talk, but what can I say, I'm not a patient man," he chuckled. "I was just sitting here thinking how nice it would be if I were in the company of a beautiful woman. Naturally, you came to mind."

"Well, aren't you the silver-tongued devil? Again, thanks for the compliment, but I'm in a lousy mood and probably wouldn't provide any decent conversation."

"Why don't you let me be the judge of that? Meet me at Fleming's Steakhouse over by the mall, please?"

"Harrison, you seem like a nice enough guy, but—"

"Then give me just a little bit of your time. We'll eat, share a nice bottle of wine and hopefully, some good conversation. C'mon, the worst that can happen is that you'll enjoy a delicious meal compliments of yours truly. Besides, the stars are out and you shouldn't waste this Saturday night on some predictable Lifetime movie."

Rozalla smiled and thought that he did make a good point. Besides, no one else was interested in spending time with her. Hell, her kids weren't even speaking to her. "Okay, you've convinced me. I can be there by nine o'clock, is that okay?"

"That's perfect," Harrison replied gleefully. "See you then."

An hour and a half later, Rozalla walked into Fleming's looking like a million bucks. She walked confidently in her beautiful maxi dress and strappy heels. She figured since she'd agreed to go out, she'd may as well look good doing it.

Her curly locks resting gently on her shoulders and understated make-up made her look radiant. Rozalla may have felt like an emotional wreck, but she looked like the queen bee. She hadn't realized that Harrison was standing in the corner of the lobby watching her as she glided in. When he stepped to her, she was in awe of him. Harrison reminded her of JFK Jr., tall, tanned, and tantalizing.

"I know you're tired of hearing this, but you look gorgeous," Harrison said with an outstretched hand.

Rozalla took his hand in hers, accepting his gentle handshake. "You clean up pretty well yourself."

"Your table is ready. Please follow me," the petite hostess instructed. She led them to an intimate, dimly lit corner table. "Is this table to your liking?"

"Yes, it's perfect," Harrison replied.

She wasn't sure if it was the wine, the food, atmosphere, or the combination of it all, but Rozalla was having a magnificent time. The conversation flowed as if they were old friends. They talked about their families, hobbies, and their careers. She was pleased to hear that he was gainfully employed as a financial advisor. Rozalla was even happier to learn that he was a divorcee. It meant that he knew how difficult it was to make a relationship work. Maybe now he'd be willing to put in the work to create something beautiful with her. The night ended with Harrison walking her to her car. A warm hug and a gentle kiss was the cherry on top of this delicious date.

Within seconds of pulling out of the parking lot, Rozalla was dialing Heather's number. She was so anxious to talk to her friend that she could barely concentrate on the road. The four rings it took for Heather to pick up the line seemed like an eternity.

"Hey girlie, what's up?"

"Heather, I think I'm in love."

"What the hell are you talking about? Who are you in love with?"

"Harrison," Rozalla gushed. "He is all kinds of sexy and a great conversationalist. I swear, this was the best time I've had in years."

"Okay, who is Harrison and where have you been? I didn't know anything about you going out tonight."

"C'mon, you remember the guy from Tin Lizzy's? You said he tricked me into giving him my number."

Heather's voice must have risen three octaves. "O-M-G, I can't believe you went out with him. Give me details, I want to hear it all. Don't leave out a thing."

Maneuvering her car through the city, Rozalla recounted every detail of her time with Harrison. The entire time she talked, she never stopped smiling and only realized it once her cheeks started to ache. She didn't care though, it was the best kind of ache. She continued the conversation long after she'd made it home. The more they talked, the more Heather wanted to hear. This went on until Rozalla had recounted every detail at least twice.

"Okay girl, I'm all talked out," Rozalla announced. "I'm going to run a bubble bath, pour myself a glass of wine and relax. We'll talk tomorrow or Monday. Good night."

She did just as she'd said she would and relaxed into a hot tub of water. Her favorite Jazz music was playing in the background and the wine was arousing her in a manner she hadn't experienced since well before Vince had died. She began to caress her breasts, gently squeezing her erect nipples. Her hand wondered down until it found her pleasure spot. She began to lustfully massage that special place as fantasies of Harrison seducing her danced in her head. She imagined her hand was his and that his tongue was dancing with hers. As her fingers stroked in and out, her breathing hastened until finally, she reached her climax. Rozalla's body relaxed back into the water as she thought of how much better that would've been had Harrison really been there.

CHAPTER TWELVE

The last month had been great for Rozalla. She and Harrison were now deep into a seemingly loving relationship. When they weren't at work, they were with one another. They'd even double-dated with Heather and her flavor of the month. Now, Rozalla really wanted her girls and Amanda to meet him. She wanted the three of them to share in her new-found happiness. She'd reached back out to each of them and felt relieved that they'd all been open to rebuilding the close relationship they all once shared. However, she wasn't sure that they'd be at all interested in seeing her with another man. She knew that it would be hard for her daughters and understandably so, but she prayed that Amanda would be supportive.

Having convinced her daughters and Amanda to come over for Sunday dinner, Rozalla found herself running around the kitchen like a mad chef. On the menu were her famous "fall off the bone" ribs, mac and cheese, green beans, corn muffins, and peach cobbler. As she sprinkled sugar over the top of her unbaked cobbler, Harrison came up behind her and wrapped his arms around her waist. Knowing the feelings it evoked, he kissed and nibbled on her neck. She moaned softly which only encouraged him to keep going. He eased her little sundress up her thighs and began to massage her sweet spot through her panties. Her juices began to soak through and Rozalla could feel Harrison's growing excitement press into her lower back. He pulled her panties to the side and his finger found its way into her sugar walls. Darting in and out, Rozalla was finding it hard to contain herself.

"We have to stop, Harrison. Everyone will be here soon," she said breathlessly.

"They won't be here for another two hours and I promise to make it a quickie." He never stopped massaging her, never stopped nibbling and kissing.

Rozalla spun around and took Harrison's tongue into her mouth. They kissed passionately as he unzipped her dress and let it fall to the floor. He bent down and began to suck her breasts, first one and then the other. He stood up and lifted Rozalla off her feet. She wrapped her legs around his waist as he walked with her into the bedroom. He quickly laid her on the bed, dropped his pants, and started moving in and out. Rozalla's moans grew with every stroke Harrison made until finally, she released all over him and he in turn released in her. It was truly the break she'd needed. But now it was time to get up, clean up and finish preparing her meal.

Lisa was the first to arrive and despite the look of shock written all over her face, she kept all of her negative thoughts to herself when she was introduced to Harrison. She had to admit that he was a handsome guy, but nothing about him appeared to be the strong type of man that her father was. The three of them made small talk and Lisa nibbled on a carrot stick as she anxiously waited for the others to arrive. Finally, the bell rang and she shot for the door like a bullet.

"Hey Ms. Amanda, please come on in," Lisa sang. She gave Amanda a big hug and whispered in her ear, "Boy, does she have a surprise for you."

Amanda took a deep breath and prepared herself for whatever Rozalla had in store. She walked through the house until she found the others in the kitchen giggling like teenagers. "Well, what do we have here?" she asked.

"Amanda, it's so good to see you!" Rozalla had to fight back tears as hugged her tightly. She'd missed their friendship more than she'd realized. "We have so much to catch up on."

"I see," Amanda replied with raised eyebrows. "So how about we start with introductions?"

"Amanda, this is Harrison. Harrison, this is my dear friend, Amanda."

Harrison stepped up and extended his hand to Amanda. "So nice to meet you, I've heard a lot of wonderful things about you."

"Nice to meet you as well. Unfortunately, I haven't heard anything about you. But I guess that's why I'm here, huh?" she said with a slight smile.

"You're here because I've missed you and my girls. I couldn't think of a better way for us to come back together than over a great meal. And yes, I did want you all to meet Harrison," Rozalla confessed.

"You know I could never pass up one of your amazing dinners, and I'm sure that the conversation will be entertaining, to say the least. Isn't that right, Lisa?"

Lisa didn't verbally answer Amanda, she simply smiled and nodded her head. It was her plan to sit back and observe. Lisa had no desire to get into a war of words with her mom or the new guy that she was trying to pawn off on them. The doorbell rang and again, she jumped to go answer it.

"Hey Carmen, how's my big sis?" Lisa asked as she offered a peck on the cheek.

Carmen returned the kiss as she scoped out the house. "Who all is here?"

"Just Ms. Amanda and Mama's special guest," Lisa replied with a hint of sarcasm.

"Aww hell, is it that damn Heather? I'm not in the mood for any drama."

"No, I promise you that it's not Heather. I think Mama finally got the message that we don't care for that female. Speaking of not caring for stuff, I don't care for the fact that you didn't return my call the other day. You better start making time for me, girl," Lisa fussed as they entered the kitchen.

"Hi Mama, hi Ms. Amanda, how are y'all doing?" Carmen asked, greeting them with hugs.

"It's so good to see you, Carmen. You all have no idea how good it feels to have everyone here. I've missed this so much." Rozalla could feel tears of joy dancing on the rims of her eyes.

"It is good to see all my girls," Amanda confessed.

"Hmm, I see that there is one gentleman joining this circle of sisters today. Who might we have here?" Carmen asked.

"Hello Carmen, I'm Harrison. It's so nice to meet you," he greeted with an outstretched hand.

Carmen took his hand in hers and smiled flirtatiously. Is he the reason Lisa had acted all weird? Had her mother arranged all this just to hook her and Harrison up? He wasn't someone that she'd normally give a second glance, but maybe her mom was on to something. He wasn't her norm, but he sure was good looking. She hadn't realized that she was still holding Harrison's hand, until Rozalla stepped in between them.

"I've been so excited for you all to meet Harrison. He's become a very special part of my life," Rozalla blushed. "We've been spending a lot of time together and he's quite important to me."

"We're important to each other, babe," Harrison added.

Carmen felt as if someone had knocked the wind out of her. She also felt foolish and it showed all over her face. She stepped back and hung her head in embarrassment.

"Oh, I had no idea."

"You're not the only one that was left in the dark, sis. None of us knew about this new found relationship," Lisa chimed in, trying to ease the awkwardness.

Amanda walked over to the stove and saw all the serving dishes filled with the delicious dinner Rozalla had prepared. "It looks like dinner is ready. When can we sit down and dig in? I'm starving."

"Right now," Rozalla sang happily. "You guys go wash up while I place the food on the table."

Everyone washed their hands and took a seat at the beautifully decorated, rectangular dining room table. Carmen was still feeling pretty foolish about the assumption she'd made earlier. She, along with everyone else, never expected for Rozalla to choose someone like Harrison. He was the polar opposite of Vince. With Rozalla finding fault in everything Vince did and said the last couple of years of his life, maybe this was what she thought she needed.

"Who wants to say grace?" Rozalla asked.

"You're the head of the house now, Mama. You should do the honors," Lisa said dryly.

Determined not to have any unnecessary drama, Rozalla had everyone hold hands and bow their heads. While her mother led the gathering in prayer, Carmen's awkward moment continued with Harrison now holding her hand. She found herself trying to figure out if he was inappropriately squeezing it. The prayer was over and as they all released their grip on one another, Harrison slowly slid his from Carmen's, pausing long enough to finger the palm of her hand. Yes, she misread the situation earlier, but she definitely wasn't misreading this. Throughout the evening, Harrison found more reasons and ways to touch or brush up against Carmen than the law ought to allow. As Rozalla recounted how she met her new love interest, he stretched his leg out, allowing it to slightly move up and down Carmen's leg.

Unable to take it any longer, Carmen excused herself from the table. She lingered in the bathroom trying to decide if she should say anything. She looked in the mirror and decided that now was not the time. She returned to the table and took the empty seat beside Lisa.

"Why did you move over there, sweetie? Did Harrison scare you away?" Rozalla joked.

"Nope, just want to sit here and annoy my baby sister."

"So what's next for you guys?" Amanda inquired.

"Yeah Mama, what's next?" Lisa chimed in. She cocked her head to the side, waiting to hear where her mom thought this little love affair was headed.

"Right now we're just really enjoying each other. It's so refreshing to have someone to go out with, experience new things with, and hopefully soon, travel with."

"Where the hell are y'all going?" Carmen hissed in a tone harsher than she intended it to be.

Rozalla looked shocked by Carmen's tone, but chose to look past it. "We are planning to head to Hawaii for an eight-day vacation next month."

Silence fell over the room like a suffocating blanket. Amanda had so many questions, but chose not to ask a thing. Carmen cleared her throat as if she were going to say something profound, but she too opted to keep silent. Lisa picked up her wine glass, took a long sip, cleared her throat, and did what everyone else was either too shocked or too chicken to do. She spoke up.

"Do you have any idea how expensive a vacation like that is? I mean if he's footing the bill for it, then cool. Do you even have that much vacation time left for this year?"

"Yes Lisa, I still have six days of vacation left and I'm going to take the additional two days without pay. And I wouldn't dare have Harrison foot the entire bill for such an expensive trip. I've already told you guys that he's a financial planner and he does investments as well. He's turned me on to short-term investments that will net me a good deal of money and allow me to pay my half of the vacation," Rozalla explained.

"Mama, I know you're not going to turn over any of the insurance money from Daddy's death or his investments to this man," Lisa said sternly.

"Lisa, it's all my money now and why wouldn't I take this golden opportunity to double it? This is, after all, what he does for a living, he makes people money," Rozalla said.

"I understand that he *told* you all of that, but have you bothered to check him out, verify that he's a decent investor, and not just another scam artist?"

"Lisa, watch your mouth! I trust Harrison implicitly. He's been nothing but kind and loving. You should be so lucky as to have someone like him in *your* life." Rozalla couldn't contain her anger and she kept ranting long after she should have shut up. "Is that the problem, you all are jealous? You're upset that you can't find a man as good as Harrison for yourselves? And the money, your father was so tight with that money that I never got to enjoy any of the real pleasures in life. Now it's my chance and I'm going to take it."

"How could you even say something like that to us, Mama?" Carmen's eyes were full of tears.

"I thought you called us here to start over, to mend the relationships with me and your children. But what just spewed from your mouth lets me know that you have no desire to mend anything. I can't believe that you would say such things to your daughters. What happened to the woman that showered her kids with love, cared for them and protected them? What happened to the friend I used to know?" Amanda questioned. "You're so consumed with living the life you think you were denied by your marriage that you've lost every drop of common sense you ever had. I love you, but I won't listen to you insult us. I won't be a witness to your self-destruction. When you find the good, kind, sensible woman that I used to know, have her call me."

Amanda grabbed her purse and headed for the door. With tears in their eyes, the girls also got up to leave.

"Wait, please wait," Rozalla begged. "I'm so sorry, I didn't mean any of that. I love y'all so much and I swear I didn't mean any of that. Please don't walk out like this," she cried, but her tears didn't slow anyone's journey to the door. "Please…"

Carmen turned and walked back to her mother. She looked Rozalla in the eye, leaned in and kissed her on the cheek. "I love you, Mama, but I can't be around you right now." She turned back around and walked out.

Lisa said nothing to her mother, but she looked at Harrison and warned, "If you take advantage of her, use her, scam her or hurt her in any way, I swear I'll hunt you down and kill you my damn self." She then snatched her keys off the side table and walked out with no intention of returning any time soon.

CHAPTER THIRTEEN

"Are you sure you don't want me to go with you, babe?"

Harrison offered for the second time. They had to make the final payment on their vacation and Rozalla was all too glad to go take the balance of what they needed out of the bank. After all, Harrison had generously paid for the majority of the trip. He'd even gone so far as to purchase her a new set of Coach Luggage. Rozalla had never owned anything that extravagant. Vince thought he was doing something big when he bought them matching luggage from Burlington Coat Factory. Finally, she had someone that gave her what she deserved.

"No sweetheart, you stay here and relax. I won't be long," she gave him a peck on the lips and headed out the door.

Rozalla jumped in her car, blasted her music and took off. She couldn't imagine anything that could bring her down off of the high she'd been on since hooking up with Harrison. He was the breath of fresh air she'd been waiting for. He wasn't afraid to spend a little money and give her the finer things that she deserved. The luggage, the trip, the Manolo Blahnic's from Atlanta's most upscale mall. Yes, he definitely spoiled her and she loved every minute of it. She knew that her girls missed their father, but if they could just see how Harrison treated her, they'd be thrilled for her.

While Rozalla was making her way to the bank, Carmen was pulling up to her mom's house. She'd spent the last couple of days in the city, and wanted to get a couple of things she'd left in her old room, before heading back to Athens. She also wanted to see if her mother was ready to make amends. Of the two girls, Carmen had always been closer to their mom and hated the stress and tension that continued to pull them apart. She knew that Rozalla was seeking the love that she felt she'd missed with Vince, but the truth of the matter was that Vince adored Rozalla and everybody knew it. What no one could understand was how Rozalla had lost sight of how much love Vince had for her.

After knocking on the door a couple of times, Carmen used her key to enter the house. She was shocked when she walked in the family room and found Harrison laid up on the couch watching television as if it was his home.

"Where is my mother?" Carmen questioned.

Harrison sat up and turned to see who had boldly walked in on him. "Carmen, hi there. Rozalla didn't tell me that you were coming over. How are you?"

"I'm fine thanks. Where is she?"

"You just missed her. I'm surprised that you guys didn't pass each other. Why don't you come around and have a seat?" Harrison patted the cushion beside him.

Carmen was annoyed that he was offering up seats as if it was his house. This was still her home too, and she didn't appreciate him acting as if it weren't. "Do you know how long she'll be gone?" She asked as she sauntered to the kitchen for a bottle of water.

"She shouldn't be long. She just made a quick run to the bank. Make yourself at home, kick your feet up, and Rozalla will be here before you know it."

"I am at home! You're the visitor here, not me," Carmen snapped.

"I'm sorry, you are completely right, Carmen. I didn't mean to insinuate anything different."

Carmen took her bottle of water and huffed off to her old room. She was bent over, rummaging through her closet, looking for a box of books she'd left behind. She hadn't heard Harrison creep up behind her and was shocked to feel his hand on the small of her back. She jumped and turned, and found herself standing nose to nose with her mother's boyfriend. "What the hell," she yelled as she shoved him back. "Why are you all up on me?"

"I'm sorry, I didn't mean to scare you. I simply wanted to talk to you, see if we can get things back on track with you and your mom."

"Next time you want to talk to me, you announce yourself and ask permission. I don't like people invading my personal space, and the fact that you're even in here feels inappropriate."

Harrison held his hands up as if to surrender. "I didn't mean to offend you or invade your space. I came in here with pure intentions. Your mom loves you and your sister so much, but she's having a hard time understanding why you two can't be happy for her."

"I'll be happy for her when she's in a situation worthy of my joy. But for now, I'll continue to pray that she's not being taken advantage of, and that you are truly a decent man."

Harrison stepped closer to Carmen, put his hand to her face and spoke sweetly. "I know you were disappointed when you found out that I was dating Rozalla. It was clear that you wanted me for yourself." He stroked her cheek again. "Yes,

I'm with Roz and I love her, but that doesn't mean that I can't spend a little satisfying time with you as well."

Carmen smacked his hand away from her face. "What the hell do you think you're doing? You low-life piece of shit, keep your hands off of me."

"Tell me I'm lying, Carmen, tell me that you didn't want me. Tell me you don't still want me." Harrison quickly moved back towards Carmen, grabbed her by the back of the head and pressed his lips to hers.

Carmen pulled away and slapped him as hard as she possibly could. "You freaking bastard! Don't you ever put your nasty ass hands on me again!" She grabbed her keys and bolted out the room towards the front door. She snatched the door open and there stood Rozalla.

"Hey baby! What a pleasant surprise, I didn't know you were coming over," Rozalla sang as she stepped into the house. Noticing the keys in her Carmen's hand, Rozalla asked, "You're not leaving are you? I just got here and you couldn't have been waiting long. Come on, sit down and talk to me for a while, please?"

With no desire to hide her anger, Carmen boldly told Rozalla what had just happened between her and Harrison. "He is a pig, Mama, and if you have the sense of a flea, you'll kick his ass out and forget you ever knew him."

"Wait, what happened?" Rozalla asked as she grabbed Carmen by the arm to try and prevent her from leaving.

"Babe, let her go. Nothing happened here. I was kidding around with her and clearly, she doesn't know how to take a joke," Harrison explained.

"So you're a liar *and* a cheat," Carmen spat. "This snake tried to kiss me, Mama. He grabbed me and kissed me on the mouth. I had to pop his ass across the face to get him away from me."

"Harrison, is this true? Did you really try and push yourself off on my daughter?"

"Why the hell are you asking him anything, Mama? I just told you what happened!" Carmen shouted.

"Babe, I told you, I was just joking. It was my feeble attempt to lighten the mood and get her to hang out and spend a little time with you," Harrison explained. "I'm truly sorry if I offended you, Carmen. What can I say, my inner comic needs a little work."

"Come on back in and spend some time with me, Carmen. We'll kick Harrison and his piss poor excuse of a comedy routine out. That way we can catch up without interruption. Harrison, you can go run those errands you'd mentioned earlier."

"Are you serious?" Carmen asked. "What I told you doesn't upset you; it doesn't even faze you, huh? So this idiot's word carries more weight than mine now. I guess he could tell you anything and as long as he keeps your bed warm at night, you'll believe him. You're pathetic," Carmen spat at Rozalla and stormed out the house.

CHAPTER FOURTEEN

Four days had passed and Rozalla still hadn't been able to get Carmen to return her calls. She realized that she probably should have been more understanding of Carmen's feelings the other day, but she truly felt like it was all a harmless joke on Harrison's part. Would anyone else see it that way and now deem her a worthless excuse of a mother? As she packed her bags for vacation, she waited for her friends to arrive. An honest opinion is what she knew she'd always get from Amanda. Yes, after her last interaction with her, Rozalla had to apologize and grovel a bit for her friend's forgiveness. Nevertheless, she knew that Amanda was too good of a friend to hold her grudge for long. Heather would also give an honest opinion, but Heather seemed to always be a little more on Rozalla's side these days and she loved that.

As Amanda pulled up to the house, another car pulled right in behind her. Within seconds, out stepped Heather. Amanda rolled her eyes in disgust and had to talk herself out of hitting the gas, running the heifer down and celebrating her demise with a cocktail. "Girl, don't let Ms. Thang make you lose your religion. Get it together," Amanda disciplined herself. She took a deep breath, said a little prayer and exited the car.

"Hey Amanda, I thought that was you," Heather sang cheerfully as she waited for Amanda to catch up so that she could wrap her up in a big hug.

"Hi Heather, how are you?" Amanda replied with an obviously fake smile and pat on the back.

"I'm great girl, how have you been?"

"Just fine, thanks." Amanda knocked on the door and prayed that Rozalla would make it to the door quickly. She was already tired of being in Heather's presence.

A broad smile covered Rozalla's face as she opened the door. "My girls," she sang. "I'm so happy to see you both. Come on in, I've got wine, fresh fruit and cheese from Publix, and plenty to talk about." She greeted them both with a hug and ushered them into the kitchen.

"So, what going on, Roz? You sounded upset on the phone when you called me. The girls are okay, aren't they?" Amanda asked.

"Funny you should ask." Rozalla poured everyone a glass of wine, took a big sip of hers, and told them what had happened between Carmen and Harrison. She explained how she truly thought that Harrison was making light of the fact that Carmen was clearly attracted to him when they first met. She went on to explain that although she thought it was no big deal, she now felt like she handled it all wrong, because Carmen was once again not speaking to her. "I swear y'all, when it comes to my daughters, I can't seem to do anything right. Not since Vince has been gone anyway. So what do you think, was I wrong?"

Amanda stood there looking at Rozalla as if she'd lost her natural mind. "You can't be serious? You've known this man for two seconds and you automatically take his word over your daughter's? Rozalla, you are smarter than this. Carmen wouldn't lie about what transpired between them, and as a woman, she knows beyond any shadow of a doubt when a man is sexually inappropriate with her. It sounds like you need to reevaluate your new relationship and apologize to your child!"

"I couldn't disagree with you more," Heather scolded. With a scowl on her face, she began to spatter her objections. "Your daughters are grown women now, not little sniveling kids that you have to run behind and protect. It's time for you to live for yourself! Your husband is gone, your kids are grown, and you have nothing to tie you down. You've met a great man that spoils you and loves you the way you deserve to be loved. Don't blow it because of a mix up or joke gone wrong."

"Are you seriously implying that Vince didn't love her the way she deserved?" Amanda asked angrily. "You didn't know him and have any idea of the life they built. If anything, Roz needs to drop to her knees and beg God to send her another man as good as Vince, because what she has now can't even come close."

"Come on ladies, let's not fight," Rozalla begged.

"I did know him and while he was nice, he wasn't the magical prince you make him out to be," Heather retorted. "Rozalla is now getting a taste of the good life. Expensive gifts, money, trips."

"If that's what you think love is then you're a fool and can expect to be alone the rest of your ignorant life," Amanda snaped.

"You bitch…" Heather spat.

"Stop it, just stop it!" Rozalla screamed. Tears began to roll down her face as she started to plead with her friends. "I called you here to help me, not to fight and call each other names. I need my friends, but what you two are doing is only making my life more difficult."

Amanda stood to her feet and gathered her purse and keys. "I love you Rozalla and I know that you love and trust your children. Carmen would never lie on Harrison in an attempt to make you leave him or just because she doesn't like him. She's not that kind of girl. But no one knows that better than you. All I can tell you now is pray about your relationship with Harrison and listen when God speaks to your heart." She kissed Rozalla on the cheek and left.

"Well thank God she's gone," Heather huffed.

"She's a great person and a wonderful friend, Heather. You just need to give yourself a chance to get to know her." Rozalla couldn't help but defend her friend.

"I know she's your friend, but so am I. As your friend, I want to see you happy and enjoying life. It's clear to see that Harrison makes you happy. Your daughters are very sensitive to everything right now. They are missing their father and trying to figure life out without him in it. But you've figured yours out, and it's not fair for you have to throw your happiness away in an effort to pacify them. You deserve this happiness."

~~~

Carmen sat in a corner booth at The Cheesecake Factory nursing a martini, waiting for Lisa and Amanda to arrive. The master plan had been for Rozalla to join them, but after the fiasco with Harrison, Carmen aborted that idea. She was still furious and couldn't believe that Rozalla still opted to go on that Hawaiian vacation with that jackass. She'd actually chosen that man over her own child. Frustrated with the entire situation, she downed the rest of her drink and ordered another one. Just as her martini arrived at the table, so did Lisa.

"Hey gorgeous, what are you drinking?" Lisa teased.

"Hey chica, you're late," Carmen scolded. "Excuse me, please bring her a martini as well," she then requested of the server.

"So we're drinking martinis today?"

"Girl, they're peach martinis, same thing as Kool-Aid. Have you heard from Ms. Amanda?"

"I'm right here," Amanda chimed as she stepped to the booth. "And again, please stop calling me Ms. Amanda. For Pete's sake, y'all are grown now, I'm simply Amanda," She fussed as she scooted in the seat next to Lisa.

"So, is Mom coming? If memory serves me well, it was your project to try and bring us all together," Lisa asked.

The server approached the table and placed the drinks in front of the ladies. Amanda ordered a daiquiri for herself and a couple of appetizers for them to share. Carmen opened her mouth to recount the mess that happened, but a large party beside them started singing happy birthday at the top of their lungs. Instead, she decided to take a couple of more sips from her drink and wait out the noise that they called singing. After the noise had ceased, Carmen continued to sip in silence.

"Hello, earth to Carmen." Lisa snapped her fingers in sister's face. "You were about to tell us if we should wait on Mom, or if she opted to pass on our little gathering."

Carmen's eyes welled up and despite her efforts, a couple of tears trickled down her cheek. "So I went over to the house the other day, and Harrison is there chilling on the couch. That bastard started talking about how he and I could still spend time together, and then he grabbed me and kissed me. I slapped the shit out of him and was about to walk out when Mom came home."

"I know she put him out," Lisa interrupted.

"No, I told her what happened, he told her he was kidding and she sided with him. So they can both kiss my ass. Any woman, who would choose some random dude over her own child, is not worth my time or my tears!" Carmen angrily dabbed at her eyes with a napkin.

"Why am I not shocked?" Lisa rolled her eyes and sucked her teeth in disgust. "Have you heard anything from her, Amanda?"

"Yes, she called me over to talk about the situation. Problem is, she invited Heather over too. She and I ended up arguing over what Rozalla should do. I got pissed, told your mom to pray about it, and I left."

Feeling hopeful, Carmen asked, "So do you know what she decided?"

"She flew out to Hawaii with Harrison this morning."

CHAPTER FIFTEEN

Rozalla gazed out of the window like a deer caught in headlights as the plane descended into Hawaii. She couldn't stop smiling, couldn't contain her joy. She realized she was still in the U.S., but the views were so breathtaking that she felt as though she'd just arrived in some exotic foreign country.

"Do you see all of this, Harrison? It's beautiful here, like we've landed in heaven."

"It is beautiful," Harrison agreed. "The only thing lovelier is you and your wide-eyed excitement. I swear babe, this week we're going to have the time of our lives. You deserve this and so do I." He stroked Rozalla's face and gently kissed her.

Shortly after their flight landed, the courtesy van from their resort picked them up and began its journey to paradise. They laughed and enjoyed the scenery along the way. An older couple in the vehicle smiled at them warmly and the lady asked, "Is this your honeymoon?"

Rozalla blushed at the thought of being married to someone as wonderful as Harrison. "No ma'am, we're dating," she confessed.

"You kids and your modern day dating. Goodness, we've been saving for years for a trip like this. If you can do all this while you're dating, what in the world will you do after you've been married for twenty years?" The lady continued.
Thankfully, her husband interjected. "Mable, leave these young people alone. Please excuse her," he addressed Rozalla and Harrison. "She's just jealous that we had to wait so long," he chuckled.

Lighthearted conversation continued between the two couples and before long, they were pulling up to the Hilton Hawaiian Village Waikiki Beach Resort. Everything about it was gorgeous. From the beautiful lawn sculptures, to the palm tree lined pathways, to the crystal clear pools, and the white, sandy beaches. It was all exquisite. Staff welcomed them with beautiful leis and fruit adorned cocktails. They checked in and the bell hop took their luggage up to their ocean view room. Harrison peeled off a five-dollar bill and tipped the guy. He then turned and starred at Rozalla for a moment as she ran through the suite commenting on the beauty of it all. When she went to the balcony and took in the amazing view, he decided to join her. He walked up behind his lady love and wrapped his arms tenderly around her waist.

"This is incredible, babe. I can't believe we were able to pull off such an extravagant vacation," Rozalla said.

Harrison moaned sensuously in her ear as his hands began to travel down and caress her curvaceous hips. He started inching up her maxi dress so that he could feel her smooth skin. Kissing and nibbling at her ear, he whispered, "I want you right here."

"On the balcony? But everyone can see us," Rozalla whimpered. "What if someone reports us for indecent exposure?" She tried to keep her composure, but as his hands roamed between her legs, she could feel her panties getting soaked.

"Look around, babe, we're on the thirtieth floor and the next building is at least a half mile away. No one will know what we're doing," Harrison assured her. He lifted her dress further and began to fondle her breasts, firmly squeezing her nipples. Her moans were his permission to continue.

Harrison was not a selfish lover. It was always his goal to make sure that Rozalla was completely satisfied, before he even thought about allowing himself to release. He moved his hands back down her body and slid her panties down to her ankles. He kneeled down and freed her feet from the constraint of the undergarment. Sitting down and turning his back to the balcony, Harrison positioned himself perfectly between her legs and began to feast on her sweet juices. He licked and sucked her clit, darted his tongue in and out of her sugar walls until she couldn't hold it any longer, and her juices poured out over his face. Rozalla thought that Harrison would rush to get away from her eruption, but it excited him even more. He separated her lips with his fingers, licking and suckering feverishly until more oozed from her kitten. Once he was confident of her complete satisfaction, he stood to his feet, dropped his pants and entered Rozalla from behind. His gentle entrance quickly turned into powerful thrusting. Rozalla could feel every inch of him pounding into her warm, wet flesh.

"Faster," she moaned, and he was glad to give her what she wanted. Harrison pounded in and out until she cried out. Then and only then, did he allow himself to release inside of her. The two collapsed onto the chaise that adorned the balcony and enjoyed the view for a while longer.

CHAPTER SIXTEEN

Amanda's new coworker was handsome, comical, but about an inch and a half shorter than she was. And that was without heels. He asked Amanda out on a date at least once a day and today would be no exception. Amanda didn't mind though, Nathan was an incredibly sweet man and always asked in a joking manner. If he would magically grow a little, she'd take him up on one of his offers.

"Good morning, beautiful, how are you today?" Nathan peeked his chocolate, handsome face with its perfectly shaped goatee into her office.

"I'm just peachy, Nathan, how are you today?"

"If I could enjoy this view all day, I'd be perfect," he replied with a wink. "Do you have a minute? I need to get your opinion on something."

"Sure, come on in." Amanda was loving her new position as an Insurance Case Manager. It put her on the corporate side of healthcare, and she was enjoying it and all the new responsibilities that accompanied it. Sadly, Rozalla had been so caught up in her new man that Amanda hadn't even had a chance to share the good news of her new position with her.

Nathan sat in the chair across the desk from Amanda and adjusted his suit jacket. "I've got this patient with cancer. It started as lung cancer, but it's now stage four and has spread throughout her body. Her husband is literally begging for us to cover her visit to M.D. Anderson Hospital. He's gotten the company, Angel Flight, to fly her to Texas for free. We both know that this is a phenomenal waste of money and resources, but how do I tell him no? This man is desperate to save his wife's life," he said sympathetically.

"I don't think you should tell him no. I know it's a costly call to make, but sometimes we have to look beyond the budget. If there is the slightest chance that they could offer life saving measures, we have to give them the opportunity to do so. Besides, M.D. Anderson does a thorough evaluation first, and if they really feel there's no hope, they won't offer any treatments or surgeries."

"See, that's why I come to you. You're always insightful and know how to get things done within these rigid guidelines." Nathan stood to his feet and moved to the other side of the desk. Yes, it was time for him to once again extend the invitation for a date. "So, I've got these tickets to the Jill Scott concert Saturday night at Chastain Amphitheater. We could go out for an early dinner, then grab a fantastic bottle of wine to enjoy at the concert. What do you say?"

"Oh wow, I love Jill Scott," Amanda sang more enthusiastically than she meant to. Aside from the fact that he was shorter than she was, she had serious doubts about dating a co-worker. "Can I let you know tomorrow?"

"I suppose so." Nathan was a little disappointed that she didn't immediately accept, but at least she didn't flat out say no. As he went to stand from the corner of her desk, he noticed her computer screen. "Don't tell me that you're interested in that guy?" His tone was as if the man on the page was the devil.

"Oh hell no! He's actually dating my best friend. I've been skeptical of him from the beginning and thought I'd Google him and see if anything suspicious came up."

"Well what did you find?"

"Nothing yet," Amanda sighed. "I guess he's okay after all."

"Yeah right, do me a favor and type in the name Joseph Cambridge. That's his real name, let's see if it's caught up to him yet."

Amanda did as she was told. As soon as the page loaded, all of the color drained from her face. How could this be? How had Rozalla gotten caught up with someone like this? Joseph Cambridge, aka Harrison, was a wanted man. According to several new reports, Harrison had swindled several women out of hundreds of thousands of dollars. There were charges of theft by deception, forgery, and the worse one, aggravated assault.

Shaking her head in disbelief, Amanda asked, "How did you know about him?"

"That aggravated assault charge is a result of the severe beating he gave my sister after she found out he'd stolen five-thousand dollars from her account and threatened to call the cops. My advice to you is to hurry up and warn your friend. Her life could depend on it."

CHAPTER SEVENTEEN

Rozalla tossed pillows from the sofa, looked through the drawers and felt under the covers of the bed, but still couldn't find her cell phone. She'd tried calling it from the room phone, but didn't hear it ringing.

"Harrison, have you seem my phone? I can't find it anywhere and wanted to make sure you hadn't seen it before I call hotel security."

"I took it," he mumbled.

"Why would you take my phone? I need to be able to check in with my girls."

"Your girls are grown. Amanda started blowing your phone up last night. All that ringing woke me up, so I took the phone and shut it off."

"Oh, sorry it disturbed your sleep, but you can give it back now. I need to make sure that there wasn't some type of emergency."

"No," Harrison replied bluntly.

"What do you mean, no? Give me my phone, Harrison, now!"

Harrison yanked out her phone, fumbled with it and threw it at Rozalla as if he were trying to take her head off with it. Luckily she ducked and it bounced off the wall, landing on the carpet. Rozalla looked at him as if he'd lost his natural mind.

"What in the hell is wrong with you?" she snapped as she picked up her phone. "You know what, Harrison, I don't have time for your games. Give me the damn battery."

"This is our vacation, Rozalla. I didn't drop all this money for you to spend all your time on the phone with those idiots back home. It's bad enough that I've had to listen and be embarrassed by you for the last two days, oohing and ahhing at everything as if you've never been anywhere or done anything. I mean damn, do you have to fall all over the palm trees like they're the newest invention? And please, try eating a meal without smacking, talking and licking your damn fingers."

"Not once have I used my phone and forgive me for enjoying myself. I thought that was the point of the whole trip. But, forgive me, I'll keep my mouth shut and my thoughts to myself. Now give me my battery."

Harrison tossed the battery to her. She slid it back in her phone as she mumbled, "You freaking asshole."

"What did you call me?"

"Nothing," Rozalla retorted.

"You lying bitch, you called me an asshole," Harrison spat as he jumped up in her face. "Look at me! Do you see an asshole?" he screamed in her face.

Not backing down, Rozalla spoke through gritted teeth, "I see a big, worthless jackass."

Harrison turned as if he were going to walk away and without warning, he turned back and clocked Rozalla in the face, knocking her into the wall. She was visibly dazed as she slid down the wall trying to regain her bearings. She shook her head from side to side to understand the words that she was being assaulted with. Everything seemed to have an echo, as if she was hearing them through a tunnel. When she looked up, she saw Harrison throwing things around the room like a child throwing an epic tantrum. She reached up to rub her right ear and try to stop it from ringing; all she felt was wetness. Looking at her hand, she realized that it was covered in the blood that oozed from her ear. What had he done to her? Better yet, what had she done to herself? How could she have been so misled?

"I've got to get out of here," she mumbled as she tried to stand to her feet. When Harrison realized she was up and moving, he went over and punched her again, and slammed her to the ground. This time it was her nose that dripped like a faucet. *Oh God, he broke my nose*, she thought. She stayed on the floor, and began to concoct an escape plan. She didn't know how someone so loving and gentle could, without warning, turn into a mad man. What she did know was that she had to get the hell away from him. She watched as he sat on the foot of the bed and dropped his head in his hands.

"I'm sorry, Harrison. I never should've called you out of your name. And I know I shouldn't have seemed so ungrateful. I know that you were just trying to keep the stresses of our everyday life away so that we could fully enjoy this vacation."

She seemed to have reached him, because he moved to where she was and looked her in the face with sympathetic eyes. "That's all I wanted, babe. We deserve to enjoy ourselves without interruption." He caressed her face. "Oh wow, you're really bleeding. Let me get you a wet towel."

His walk to the bathroom was interrupted by a knock at the door. He stood still for a moment, hoping that whomever it was would go away. Instead, the knocking became more intense. Harrison looked at Rozalla, still in a heap on the floor and raised his finger to his lips as if to say shhh. "Be quiet babe, I'd hate for you to get any worse than you already are," Harrison threatened. He journeyed to the door. "Who is it?"

"Hotel security. We've gotten reports of excessive noise, possibly fighting coming from this room."

Harrison barely cracked the door, blocking access to the room. "I can assure you, sir, there has been no fighting in here. I'm sorry for the noise, but my girlfriend and I tend to get a little loud, if you know what I mean," he said with a wink and a smile.

While he tried to convince security, Rozalla tried to work up the nerve to scream out for help. Unfortunately, she waited too long. By the time she mustered up the courage, the officer had turned to walk away. "Help me, help me please," she called out. The officer stopped in his tracks and looked back, but Harrison had closed the door and was giving Rozalla a death stare. Without hearing another sound, the security officer went on about his business.

Harrison walked back over to Rozalla and stooped down so that they were face-to-face. "I thought I asked you to be quiet. Now I see that I can't trust you." He kissed her, grabbed her by the hair and slammed her head into the wall, knocking her out.

CHAPTER EIGHTEEN

Carmen almost hit Lisa's car as they both jockeyed for the parking space outside of Amanda's office. Lisa honked her horn while laughing at her sister's silliness. She then whipped her car into a space a few feet from Carmen and jumped out of the car.

"Girl, don't play with me like that. I would be devastated if anything happened to my big body Benz," Lisa joked as she starred lovingly at her old Honda Civic. "What are you doing here anyway?"

Carmen kissed her baby sister and responded, "Amanda told me that she had something really important to discuss with me."

"Yeah, I got the same message. I wonder what's going on."
"Only one way to find out," Carmen replied. "Let's head on in. Besides, it's hot as hell out here."

They chatted idly as they rode up on the elevator and waited for Amanda to step out of her office and get them from the reception area. "So, do you and Ashton have any plans for the weekend?" Lisa asked.

Ashton was Carmen's boyfriend of three years. For a minute, she thought they're relationship wouldn't last, but thankfully, they'd worked through their issues and were happily in love again. Carmen thought it was foolish to seek counseling when they weren't even married. But Ashton, not knowing what else to do, suggested couples therapy as a last ditch effort to hold on to Carmen. In her mind, he'd lied to her and while things hadn't gotten physical, he'd had an emotional affair with some little college girl. She'd just happened to walk in on them before they could actually do the deed.

She remembered Ashton jumping to his feet and running after her as she hastily left his Athens home. As he begged her forgiveness, the young girl rushed outside demanding that Ashton return to their date. Imagine the girl's surprise when he told her to get her shit and leave. For Carmen, that was another strike against him. Ashton had clearly planned to use the girl for sex. So not only was he a cheater and a liar, he was a dog for treating the girl the way he did. However, she finally caved in; they got counseling, began rebuilding their trust, and the couple had been good ever since.

"We're going to catch that new, Straight Outta Compton, movie and then meet another couple for a late dinner. What about you? Are you going to pull your head out of the books long enough to have a little fun this weekend?"

"Probably not," Lisa shrugged. "I've got a couple of midterm exams that I need to study for. Unless you call me and say that the movie was amazing. If so, I might sneak out for a Sunday matinee."

Amanda's office door opened and a handsome guy with a smooth goatee exited. He smiled at them sweetly as he walked past, nodding his hello. "Hi ladies, come on in," Amanda said as she stepped to the side, allowing them entry. Once they were both seated, she closed the door and took a seat behind her desk. "How are y'all doing today?"

"We're fine, Amanda, how are you?" Carmen asked.

"She's fine, but I'm curious," Lisa chimed in. "Don't get me wrong, I'm always glad to see you, but your message left me with a weird vibe."

"Well, first of all, I'm fine, Carmen, thanks for asking. And you're very perceptive, Lisa. You should have a weird vibe." Amanda adjusted herself in her chair as she tried to figure out the best way to state her concerns. "So, the guy that just left my office shared some interesting information with me the other day. I was curious about Harrison and decided to Google him. When Nathan saw his picture, he had me look him up by another name. Harrison's real name is Joseph Cambridge; he's a thief and an abuser." Amanda pulled up his mug shot and arrest record for the girls. They were devastated.

"Oh my goodness, what has Mom gotten herself into?" Carmen asked rhetorically. "We've got to warn her, y'all, we need to call her now."

"That's just it, I've been calling her for the past three days, but all I get is her voicemail. I even broke down and called that idiot, Heather, to see if she'd heard from Rozalla. She got a call once they landed and said that they only spoke for about three minutes. Rozalla gave her the name of the resort, said it was beautiful and that she'd talk to Heather later. That was the first and last she's heard from Roz," Amanda explained.

Lisa rumbled through her purse and retrieved her cell phone. "What's the name of the resort, Amanda?"

"Sweetie, I've already called the resort and left multiple messages on their room phone and with the front desk."

Lisa twisted her mouth and furrowed her brow as if she were deep in thought. "Do you still have the number?"

"Of course," Amanda answered as she slid the paper with the resort's number and address across the desk to Lisa.

Lisa dialed the number on the paper. "Yes, I'm trying to reach Rozalla Harper. She's a guest there, and we have a family emergency, but haven't been able to reach her. Can someone please go to her room and check to see if she's there?"

"Please hold one moment," the desk clerk asked. She placed Lisa on hold for a few seconds and then came back to the phone. "Ma'am, her travel companion, Mr. Payne, just happened to be walking through the lobby. I have him here if you'd like to speak to him."

"Yes please, put him on the phone," Lisa instructed.

"Hello," Harrison sounded annoyed.

"Harrison, this is Lisa. I'm looking for my mother. We've been calling for days and haven't been able to reach her. Is she okay and can you please get her on the phone?"

"Of course she's okay, she's relaxing. Or at least trying to relax, but y'all won't leave her alone long enough for her to enjoy herself," he snapped.

"Look, we've got a family emergency and really need to talk to her. Now get her on the phone!"

"Lisa, she is a million miles away and can't do anything about your damn emergency. She'll be back home tomorrow night. Until then, leave us the fuck alone." Harrison slammed down the phone, and walked away from the front desk.

"Oh my gosh, I swear I could kill that arrogant son-of-a-bitch. He says that they'll be home tomorrow night and any emergencies can wait until then. And you know what, there's not a damn thing we can do now but wait," Lisa huffed in anger.

They stayed and talked to Amanda a little while longer. The women made a pact that they would all gather at Rozalla's house tomorrow evening, and wait for her arrival. Her flight got in at 8:30 p.m. and she should make it home within forty-five minutes of landing. The girls' minds were spinning, wondering if their mom was okay, if she was in any danger, had she been hurt. Alternately, they wondered if she was really so selfish that she didn't want to take two minutes out of her vacation to speak to them. At this point, they no longer knew what to think of Rozalla.

CHAPTER NINETEEN

Harrison pranced into the resort gift shop as if he didn't have a care in the world. He walked around and gathered a couple of bottles of water, snacks and ZzzQuil Nighttime Sleep-Aid. He placed everything on the counter and pulled his wallet from his back pocket. The cashier began to ring him up and couldn't help but comment on his purchases.

"You must have a lot of trouble sleeping," she remarked. "You've bought a bottle of this stuff almost every day."

"Well, aren't you the observant one. Do you always keep track of what all the guests purchase?"

"Only the handsome ones," the young lady flirted.

"No offense, love, but you aren't pretty or wealthy enough to flirt with the handsome ones," Harrison said nastily.

The cashier gave him a death stare, threw his purchases in a bag and swiped his key card. She turned her back to him and resumed the task she was doing before he approached the counter.

"Not going to wish me a good day?" he asked sarcastically.

"I only wish you death," she spat back without turning to face him.

"That could get you fired, little girl."

"And if you die, it would be worth it," she said without hesitation, and this time she looked him in the eye so he'd know that she was serious.

Harrison took his bag and laughed as he left he shop. He'd blocked out everyone and everything around him as he walked through the lobby towards the elevators. He didn't even hear the older couple from the shuttle bus calling out to him. But they caught up with him as he waited for the elevator.

"Hello there," the older gentleman greeted him with a smile. "How are you and your lady friend enjoying these last couple days of your trip?"

"We're having a great time, thanks."

"I've seen you around, but I haven't seen that pretty girl of yours in a couple of days. She should really be out enjoying the beautiful weather."

"She's been out, I guess you just haven't seen her. Besides, she prefers spending time in the spa," Harrison explained as he pushed the button for his floor.

The couple stepped in the elevator behind him. "Will you press six please?" the lady asked as she steadied herself on her husband's arm. "So tell me, young man, do you plan to marry that pretty girl."

"Look lady, I don't think that any of that concerns you. You're asking too many questions, and need to mind your own business," Harrison snapped.

"Boy, I don't give a damn what you think of my wife, but you will not disrespect her. She was only trying to be polite and make conversation," the gentleman snapped and he turned to face Harrison eye-to-eye. Like most cowards do when they are challenged, he backed down and apologized. The man moved back closer to his wife and held her hand as they exited the elevator.

Harrison shook his head in disgust at the old couple and mumbled to himself, "Old man, I will take you and that nosey ass woman out of this world." The elevator moved on up and Harrison jumped off on the thirtieth floor. Just a few feet down the hall and he was at their door. He pulled out his key card, opened the door, and was pleased to find Rozalla just waking up. "Did you have a good nap?" he asked as he sat the bag of snacks on the desk.

It took every bit of strength Rozalla had to push herself up into a sitting position. She rubbed her face and slowly shook her head in an attempt to shake off the cobwebs. Everything was so cloudy, like she'd been in a fog for days. "What day is it?" she asked.

"It's Friday, my love. We have one more day in paradise and then it'll be time to return home. Are you hungry?"

"Yes, and thirsty. My mouth is so dry," she mumbled.

"Good thing I bought you this water. Oh, and I got some of that Smartfood popcorn you like, as well as some Oreos. Doesn't that sound delicious?"

"Harrison, I need a real meal, some vegetables and protein. I'm so weak and tired that I can hardly hold my head up. Please, I need something of substance. Why don't you let me take a shower and we go out for something? Let's enjoy this last night together," she pleaded.

"Why? So you can run and tell somebody that I hit you or drugged you? I'll pass."

"Babe, I promise not to do any of that. Look at me, I bet the bruising is gone, isn't it? No one will be able to look at me and tell that we had a scuffle. That's all it was, just a little scuffle. Please, let's go out and enjoy a good meal and some fresh air?" Rozalla was saying whatever she needed to in order to get out of that room. He'd been force feeding her heavy doses of ZzzQuil for days, keeping her knocked out. She thought that this was her only chance to get out. She was afraid of what he might do to her as their departure time approached. Right now, she'd say anything to ensure that she was on that flight home.

Harrison walked over to her, placed his hand under her chin, and lifted her face up towards his. "Aww, babe, your nose is all crooked and that cut on your lip still hasn't healed. Sorry, but your gourmet meal isn't worth me risking my freedom. But if you're a good girl, I promise to bring you back a nice chef salad. How's that?"

"It's not good enough! This isn't the vacation I paid all that money for. I deserve better than to be treated like some dog on a leash," she spat as she pulled at the handcuff that was secured around her ankle. She wasn't even sure when it had happened, but this fool had tied a rope between two pair of handcuffs. He locked one end around her ankle and the other to the foot of the bed. There was just enough rope to allow her access to the bathroom. He'd kept her drugged and would come back to the room every few hours to get her up, and sit her on the toilet. He'd give her more medication and leave again. What Rozalla didn't know was that her captor was enjoying everything that the island had to offer. Including the single women. Harrison had slept with at least two other women in the few days they'd been there.

"You are a dog, you're my little bitch," he laughed.

"Yeah, well I'm not half the bitch that your punk bitch ass is." Her anger slipped out before she could catch it. Next thing she knew, Harrison had stomped over to her and elbowed her in the face. Rozalla cried out in agony. She began to scream in hopes that someone would hear her and burst through the door to help. Sadly, no one came and before she could scream again, he smacked her in the mouth and went to retrieve the ZzzQuil.

"I knew you wouldn't act right. I can't trust you in the confines of this room, let alone out in public." Harrison ripped the protective wrapping off of the bottle and unscrewed the top.

"I'm sorry, Harrison. Please don't give me any more of that. I haven't even eaten yet. Please don't do this. I'm sorry, I swear I'll behave, if you'll just let me eat and bathe. Please Harrison," Rozalla begged, but her pleas weren't acknowledged. Harrison straddled her, holding her arms under his knees. He poured the syrup in her mouth. She began to spit it out, but then he pinched her nose closed, forcing her to swallow. He must have given her half the bottle and before he could get in the shower, Rozalla was knocked out.

It was around 2:30 p.m. Saturday afternoon when housekeeping found Rozalla still chained to the bed and sleeping. Her breathing was so shallow that for a second, the maid thought she might be dead. Harrison was nowhere to be found. He'd taken the plane tickets, all of Rozalla's cash and credit cards and disappeared without a trace. Hotel security called for the police, an ambulance, and the emergency contact tucked in Rozalla's wallet.

As medics prepared to whisk Rozalla away, the police began to question the maid that found her as well as other members of the hotel staff. The story was the same from each member of housekeeping. They all admitted to flirting with Harrison, reporting on how incredibly charming he was. One even admitting to sleeping with him in one of the vacant rooms. All of them followed his instructions to not enter his room. He told them that his traveling partner was working and had no desire to be bothered. He had them leave fresh towels and linen outside the door and no one was ever to remove or ignore the *Do Not Disturb* sign. Between the flirting and the generous tips, each housekeeper was more than willing to honor his requests.

As Rozalla was wheeled through the lobby, the elderly couple saw her and the woman began to cry. One of the officers saw the lady's reaction and asked for a moment of her time. The couple followed the officer to a nearby couch and shared with him the first conversation they had with Harrison and Rozalla. They conveyed how happy and in love they seemed, but then revealed how nasty Harrison was during their last encounter. Once they'd answered all of the officer's questions, the couple held hands and bowed their heads in prayer for Rozalla.

CHAPTER TWENTY

Amanda was walking to her car with her hands full of bags. She'd treated herself to a mini shopping spree at Saks Fifth Avenue. She figured it was time to splurge a little bit. She'd been working so hard and tirelessly that she'd earned this treat. Or at least that's what she'd told herself in an effort to rationalize the amount of money she'd just spent. Hell, if she didn't spoil herself who would? Just as she clicked the button on her car remote to unlock the door, her cell phone rang. Amanda hurriedly tossed her bags in the back seat and snatched out her cell.

"Hello."

"Is this Amanda Niles?"

"Yes it is. Who's calling?"

"This is Detective Rowlings of the Honolulu Police Department. There's been an incident involving Rozalla Harper and she had you listed as her emergency contact."

"Oh God, what's happened? Is she okay?"

"Ma'am, she's been transported to a local hospital with some serious injuries. You may want to send a family member here to be with her as she recovers. There is an ongoing investigation into what exactly happened to her," the detective assured.

"I know what happened to her, that damn Harrison Payne happened. Is he there? Have you locked him up?" Amanda asked as tears welled in her eyes.

"We suspect that he's fled the area. But rest assured, we're doing everything in our power to track him down."

Amanda plopped down behind the wheel of her car. "I can't believe this has happened. Please give me the name and number of the hospital that Rozalla's been admitted to?" After the detective gave Amanda all of the information on Rozalla, she assured him that she'd be on the next plane to Hawaii.

Amanda sat for a few minutes more, trying to figure out her next move. Should she call the girls and see if they wanted to go with her to be by her mother's side? Should she go alone and try to get a better idea of all that had transpired before breaking the news to them? She shook her head in an effort to gather her thoughts, but her head continued to spin. She needed someone to help her gain a clear perspective. Amanda started the car, dialed a number on her phone, and waited for him to pick up as she pulled away.

"Hello."

"Nathan, I'm sorry to interrupt your weekend, but I could really use your help right now," Amanda sobbed.

"Where are you?"

"I just pulled out of Phipps Plaza."

"Okay, there's a Wild Wings Café across the street. Go over there and wait for me," Nathan instructed. "I'll be there in twenty minutes."

It was the fastest twenty minutes Amanda had ever seen. It seemed that by the time she got to the restaurant, got a seat and ordered a drink, Nathan was rushing through the door.

He hurried over to the table and took a seat across from Amanda, taking her hands in his.

"What's wrong and what can I do to help?" he asked sincerely.

Amanda recounted the conversation she had with the police detective. She cried for her friend as she imagined the very worse. "What if she's dead and they didn't want to tell me over the phone? How am I supposed to tell her daughters? Nathan, they will be devastated."

"I need you to reel it back in, Amanda. You're about to have the woman buried and gone. For now, let's take the detective at his word, and accept that your friend has been hurt. We also need to call her daughters. It's not fair to keep any of this from them. And lastly, we need to book you all some airline tickets."

"Thank you, Nathan, this is why I called you. I needed someone to think rationally." Amanda pulled out her phone and called Carmen and Lisa. She relayed the call she'd received earlier and began to cry again when she heard her best friend's children sob over the phone. While she talked to them, Nathan looked for available flights to Honolulu. Luckily, there was one leaving at 7:00 a.m. the next morning. Lisa and Carmen said they'd pack a small bag and meet later that night at Amanda's house. It just made sense for them to be together, comfort one another, and drive together to the airport.

The girls were surprised to see that Amanda's co-worker was at her place when they arrived later that evening. Lisa noted that he was a handsome man, had a nice body, but didn't seem like Amanda's type. *Hell, maybe everyone needed to take a step away from what was viewed as their type*, she thought. He seemed like a genuinely nice guy and that's exactly what Amanda needed in her life. The women were formally introduced to Nathan, and he shared with them how he came to know the monster that they knew as Harrison. He spoke of how Harrison robbed his sister blind; he told them how Harrison beat her once she'd discovered what a thief he really was.

"So, Nathan, may I ask how he was able to get away? I mean, why isn't he locked up?" Lisa asked.

"He was. My sister immediately called the cops and he was arrested the very next day. But with the help of his mother, he was able to bond out of jail. Unfortunately for her, he skipped bail. The bum never showed up for his trial and subsequently, his mother lost the home she'd put up for his bail. Only a no-good punk would allow his mother to be put out on the street. Poor lady had lived in that house for thirty-seven years," Nathan explained.

"So he's just been hiding out right here in Atlanta. In plain sight," Carmen mumbled. She was in shock as to how her mother, of all people, would be the one to hook up with a sick ass bastard like Harrison. "Is Mama reaping what she's sown?" Carmen's question was almost inaudible, but Lisa still managed to hear it.

"Absolutely not!" Lisa hissed. "I know I've given Mama a hard time and haven't cared for the choices she's made, but she's done nothing to deserve this. I get that she wanted to move on with her life, and I'm still pissed at how she chose to do it. I'm even angrier at how she treated Daddy over the past few years, but no woman deserves to be physically attacked by any man."

"You're absolutely right, Lisa. No woman deserves that," Nathan agreed.

"I'm sorry, I'm just trying to think through this the same as y'all. You know how much I love Mama, and this is the last thing I'd ever want to have happen. I guess I'm just trying to understand how this could happen," Carmen sobbed.

Amanda got up from her seat and went to be by Carmen's side. She sat on the sofa and wrapped her arms around Carmen as if she were a little girl. She rocked her while she sobbed for her mother and the choices she'd made. It wasn't long before a sniffling Lisa rested on the floor and laid her head in her sister's lap. The three of them realized that the best thing they could do now was be there for Rozalla. She would need their strength, their understanding and most of all, their love. Seeing the women console one another, Nathan decided that this was the perfect time for him to ease out the door, and leave them to sort out their feelings and prepare for their early morning flight. He didn't say anything to anyone, but Amanda looked up at him just as he placed his hand on the doorknob. He returned her gaze, blew her a kiss, and slipped out the door.

CHAPTER TWENTY-ONE

The flight in to Honolulu was uneventful. The views were gorgeous, but the ladies were too preoccupied with thoughts of Rozalla to even pay attention. As soon as they disembarked from the plane, they saw a uniformed officer holding a sign with Amanda's name on it. With their carry on luggage in hand, they were whisked away to The Queen's Medical Center. The officer escorted them to a private room where Rozalla was resting. When they eased the door open, Rozalla turned her head to see who was there, and her girls could hardly hold it together. Her nose was swollen and sat crookedly on her face. Her eyes were severely bruised, and her bottom lip had been busted. It looked as if she'd gone twelve rounds Mike Tyson. Once she was able to focus and see that it was Amanda and her girls, Rozalla burst into tears. They all rushed to her side and the four women cried together.

"How could I have been so stupid?" Rozalla asked over and over again.

"You weren't stupid," Amanda assured her. "There was no way to know that Harrison was a sick ass animal. He is a wolf in sheep's clothing, preying on vulnerable women. You couldn't have known."

The doctor entered the room and joined the ladies at Rozalla's bedside. "How are we feeling today?" he asked with a smile and a gentle squeeze of his patient's hand.

"Aside from feeling like an idiot, I suppose I'm feeling a little better than I did yesterday," Rozalla replied.

"I think the coward that did this is the idiot," the doctor assured her. "I know it doesn't seem like it now, but you're actually pretty lucky that the injuries and poisoning weren't any worse than they were."

"Wait, she was poisoned too?" Lisa asked.

The doctor looked at Rozalla for permission to speak in front of everyone, and she nodded her head yes. "These are my daughters and my best friend. Anything you say to me, you can say to them."

"In that case, yes. Ms. Harper was poisoned by an overdose of a sleep aid. There were toxic amounts of diphenhydramine HCI in her system. She also suffered a broken nose that will eventually require surgery, and a busted ear-drum. As you can see, she did require a few stitches in a small cut on her cheek, and there's a lot of bruising. I anticipate that she'll be able to leave here by Tuesday, and follow up with her personal physician back home."

Lisa and Carmen asked a couple more questions of the doctor before he left the room to check on other patients. They were still trying to wrap their heads around all that he'd said when Detective Rowlings waltzed into the room. After a brief introduction, the detective began to ask Rozalla a series of questions. He wanted to know if she knew where Harrison lived, if she'd ever met any of his family and if so, had she been to their homes. He asked about Harrison's work, had she been to his office, met any of his coworkers, or seen any of his credentials. The detective asked about Harrison's finances, if he flaunted his money, or if he even had any. Amanda, Carmen, and Lisa were dumbfounded with how little Rozalla actually knew about Harrison. They were baffled as to how she could get so caught up in someone she apparently knew nothing about.

It had gotten late; Rozalla was physically and mentally exhausted. Lisa, Carmen and Amanda were tired as well. The entire ordeal had wiped them out. They all spoke words of love and support to Rozalla, gave her hugs and kisses, and caught a cab to their hotel. Rozalla laid there in bed and thought of all that had happened. She reflected on the questions asked by the detective, and her inability to provide any decent answers. She then asked herself those same questions, but exchanged Harrison's name for Vince's. She smiled as she remembered every little detail about him. From day one, he'd been an open book, never hiding anything from his lady love. Unlike Harrison, Vince never asked her to cover a charge or purchase for him; instead, he'd worked hard and brought his check home. Harrison had shown himself to be a violent monster, while Vince would have killed himself before raising his hand in anger towards her. Rozalla lifted the mirror that had been placed on her bed table and gazed at herself. She reflected on how Vince would fuss over her if she so much as cut her finger. The sweet kisses he'd plant on her to ease her pain. Her eyes welled with tears, tears that burned as they began to fall freely down her face. She wasn't the beautiful, smart, strong woman that her husband had always bragged about her being. Looking in the mirror, she saw none of that, but instead starred at the fool reflected in the glass.

The last couple of days felt like a couple of years to Rozalla. All she wanted was to be released and go home. She wanted to feel safe and nowhere felt as safe as the home she and Vince had created all of those years ago. Her support system arrived a little before noon with new clothes and shoes for Rozalla. They'd gone by her hotel to retrieve her other personal items, but opted to leave the soiled clothes behind. They didn't want Rozalla to deal with memories triggered by the garments that either had droplets or large circles of blood stains. Shortly after Amanda, Lisa and Carmen's arrival, a nurse came in with discharge papers. Rozalla breathed a sigh of release, glad to be free to leave the beautiful island that had turned so ugly for her. As she was being wheeled down the hall towards the exit, Detective Rowlings appeared.

"I'm glad to see that you're looking better, Ms. Harper. I wanted to stop by and give you the name of the Atlanta detective that will work with us to track down and prosecute Harrison Payne."

"Thank you so much for all that you've done, Detective. Hopefully the next time we talk, we'll be rejoicing over the arrest of Harrison," Rozalla said with a half-smile as she took the information he'd written down for her, as well as a copy of the police report.

CHAPTER TWENTY-TWO

Within a week of arriving home, Rozalla had met with an ear, nose and throat doctor that recommended surgery to repair the damage done to her nose. It was her prayer that the surgery would return her cute little button nose to its original state. Fortunately, no surgery would be required for her ruptured ear-drum. An antibiotic to prevent infection and three months' time would heal her ear with no permanent damage. The doctor left the exam room and his nurse appeared.

"All right Ms. Harper, the doctor wants you to have this surgery as soon as possible." Looking at the physician's schedule on the iPad, the nurse suggested, "How does Monday sound? He has one open surgical spot remaining for one o'clock p.m., but you'll need to arrive at the surgical center no later than noon so that you can be prepped."

Rozalla looked at Lisa to see if she'd be available to escort her to the surgical center, just as she had today to the doctor's appointment. Lisa gently rubbed her mom's arm and nodded her head yes. "Looks like I'll be there," Rozalla confirmed to the nurse.

"All right then, I'll call you in a little while to give you the time for your pre-op on Friday. It will also take place at the surgical center, and they'll give you some paperwork with instructions to follow the day before your operation."

Lisa held Rozalla's hand the way she used to when she was a little girl, but this time, she took the lead and walked her mom out to the car. Since returning to Atlanta, Lisa and Carmen had been taking turns staying with their mom. Between them and Amanda, Rozalla was never left alone. The one person that had not been permitted to see Rozalla was Heather, but it wasn't for lack of trying. Lisa had called Rozalla's job before they'd left Hawaii and told them that she needed to take a medical leave of absence. Heather, being one of the supervisors at the hospital where Rozalla worked, got word of this and immediately started calling Rozalla's phone. It seemed that she called at least once an hour. Carmen finally got fed up, answered one of her calls and told her that Rozalla wasn't available and wouldn't be available to speak with her anytime soon. Carmen then turned off her mom's cell phone and it hadn't been back on for days. But that didn't stop Heather; she simply began calling the home number. Unfortunately, they couldn't disconnect that phone because that is how the detectives working her case stayed in contact with Rozalla.

"You know that you don't have to baby me, right?" Rozalla asked as Lisa helped her into the house, and made sure she was comfortably seated on the couch. "There isn't a thing wrong with my extremities. It's just this ugly mug that's messed up," she half-joked.

"You're still gorgeous, Mama. Broken nose and all, no other woman can hold a candle to you. Now tell me, what would you like to eat?"

Rozalla felt bad that Lisa had to go back out for food, but she was too self-conscious, too uncomfortable with her appearance to sit up in anyone's restaurant. "I would love some of O'Charley's loaded potato soup, a garden salad and those delicious yeast rolls."

"Ooh, that does sound good," Lisa licked her lips as she pulled out her cell phone. "I'm going to call it in for their curb side to go service. That way I won't have to wait too long for it, and I can get back here to you faster." She placed the order, grabbed her keys and headed for the door. "Are you sure you're comfortable being here alone for a few minutes?"

"I'll be fine, Lisa. The ladies of The Talk will keep me company until you get back," Rozalla assured her.

"Okay, I'll be back in about twenty minutes." Lisa blew her mom a kiss, walked out the door and locked it behind her.

Rozalla settled further into the couch with the TV remote in hand. She flipped through the channels for a minute, but went right back to The Talk. She loved the panel of women, they all brought something different to the table, but all meshed together quite well. And of course, Sheryl Underwood kept her laughing. She thought that Sheryl would be the perfect friend. She's not afraid to make a fool of herself, but when it's needed, she dishes out the best advice.

"Oh well, Sheryl's not here, but thank God for Amanda and my girls," Rozalla mumbled to herself as she got up to retrieve a bottle of water from the kitchen. Bottle in hand, Rozalla headed back to the couch, but halted when she heard the doorbell rang. She stood still thinking that whoever it was would just go away. Instead, they laid on the doorbell even harder. Then Rozalla heard them calling her name. She peeked through the side of the curtain to see Heather shouting her name, and banging on the door.

"What are you doing here?" Rozalla barked as she cracked the door open. "Didn't they tell you that I wasn't taking calls or visitors?"

Heather pushed her way into the house and closed the door behind her. She turned and gasped when she got a good look at Rozalla. "Oh my gosh, what happened to you? Where you in an accident? Why didn't you tell me so I could be here for you? My God, are you in pain?" Heather hit Rozalla with a barrage of questions as she dropped her purse on the coffee table.

"Look, I don't want my business all over the hospital, which is why I didn't call you or any other co-workers," Rozalla explained.

"I'm not just another co-worker, Roz, I'm your friend. And I would never tell any of those nosey ass people on the job any of your business. Now tell me what happened," Heather demanded as she escorted Rozalla to the sofa.

They sat and Rozalla cried as she remembered the vacation from hell. Heather was shocked and sickened by all that her friend had gone through, and found herself crying as well. She couldn't believe that the man who seemed to have it all and portrayed himself as such a good guy had done all those horrible things. But beyond that, she couldn't believe that Rozalla hadn't trusted her with this information, hadn't allowed her to be there as part of her support system.

"I'm so sorry, Rozalla. I never imagined that any of this would have happened. Have the police been able to track him down?"

"Not yet, but there is a detective here working with the one in Hawaii to try and track his whereabouts. I just hope that they find him before he does this to another unwitting female."

"Again, I'm so sorry that you're having to go through all of this. But why did you not want me here for you? I thought we were friends."

"Heather, it's nothing against you, this is just not something I wanted to share with anyone outside of my immediate family. It's embarrassing and I feel so humiliated. So much so that I haven't even told my parents. Only my daughters know about this mess."

"Your daughters and Amanda," Heather said with a bit of a side eye.

"Well yes, she's listed as my emergency contact and she's the one that the police notified after they found me in that freaking hotel room."

The ladies didn't hear Lisa as she let herself in through the garage. She walked lightly into the house and snooped on the conversation, while trying to contain her anger. *How dare Heather just show up here?* They'd told her in no uncertain terms that she was not wanted and that Rozalla did not need anything from her.

"I know that Amanda has been your best friend for years, but to exclude me from something this major is very hurtful. All I've tried to do was be a good friend to you, and show you that there is more to life than sitting around mourning a dead man," Heather whined.

"That dead man is my husband," Rozalla snapped. I know you meant well, but clearly, I wasn't ready for all of that."

Lisa charged around the corner, snatched up Heather's purse and shoved it at her. "It's time for you to leave. You weren't invited over. As a matter of fact, you were specifically told to keep your ass away." Lisa walked over and snatched the front door open, "Now you have to leave. Thank you for visiting and we'll let you know when and if you're welcome back."

"Lisa, don't be so rude," Rozalla scolded. "She came here with good intentions."

"That may be, Mama, but if she weren't so busy trying to make you forget Daddy and fall for anything with a penis, none of this would have happened."

"Well, excuse the hell out of me for trying to help her move on with her life!" Heather stormed out the door and didn't look back.

CHAPTER TWENTY-THREE

Thankfully the surgery had been a successful one and Rozalla was trying to return to life as usual. She'd gone shopping to put food in the house, and couldn't wait to cook herself a good meal. During this whole ordeal, she'd been eating take out every night, and was completely sick of nutritionally deprived meals. She'd also advised her job that she would return to work in one week. Now all that was left to do was sort through the enormous amount of mail that had collected while she was out of commission. She knew that most of it was junk mail because she paid her bills online. Rozalla sifted through the advertisements, magazines and flyers, but it was the American Express envelope that stopped her in her tracks. Why in the world was American Express sending a bill to Vincent? Rozalla grabbed her letter opener, ripped the envelope open, and almost had a heart attack. The statement was requesting a payment of $28,961 be made in full within thirty days.

Snatching up her phone, Rozalla began to press buttons as if her life depended on it. When the customer service agent greeted her, she had to take a moment to calm herself before she could even speak.

"Hello, is anyone there?"

"Yes, I'm here," Rozalla finally said. "I just received a statement in my husband's name for almost thirty-thousand dollars. This is clearly a fraud situation and I need to know what y'all are going to do to fix it."

"I'm sorry to hear this, ma'am. Are you on the account?"

"No, this shouldn't be an account at all."

"I understand, but may I please speak with your husband to verify with him that this account was opened in error?"

Frustration was starting to consume Rozalla. "My husband is dead. This is a fraudulent account. It was opened after his death. Are you understanding me?" she spat.

"Yes ma'am, I apologize for the miscommunication. May I please have the account number listed on the statement?"

Rozalla recited the account number. After a brief investigation, the young lady advised that she would flag the account as a fraudulent. Once Rozalla provided them with a death certificate for Vince, they would close the account, and she wouldn't be liable for any of the charges. Furthermore, all of the information would be provided to the police for them to investigate as well. Rozalla breathed a sigh of release, wrote down her case number and disconnected the call.

After making a mental note to put a copy of the death certificate in the mail tomorrow, Rozalla continued to riffle through the email. More advertisements and a couple of solicitations for pay day loans. Rozalla thought that odd. They had never taken out any loans from these "fly by night" loan companies. Vince always said they were loan sharks in disguise. Then she came across one from a company called World Finance, and unlike the others that were addressed to resident, this one was addressed to Vince. She snatched it open only to find a statement requesting a minimum payment of $350. The total loan amount was fifteen-thousand dollars. Rozalla almost passed out. This time she decided not to call them, instead she jumped in her car and drove to their neighborhood office. After explaining everything to the manager and providing a valid death certificate, the manager told her that they would go after the imposter that opened the loan with everything they had. The manager went on to show Rozalla the loan documents as well as the identification provided at the time of the loan. The copies of the Georgia driver's license and social security card looked authentic. Looking at Harrison's face attached to her husband's information, on the other hand, was sickening. It confirmed that Harrison's plan all along was to use and abuse her. How dare he try to ruin Vince's good name and credit? She was more determined than ever to make this greedy bastard pay.

Rozalla returned home, gathered all the paperwork linked to the fraudulent accounts, and called the detective working her case to set up a meeting. He agreed to see her, and advised her to continue to sort through her mail, and check all of her accounts prior to the meeting they'd scheduled for the next day. Rozalla did as she was told and was thankful that she didn't find any more open accounts. Breathing a sigh of relief, she went into the kitchen, poured a glass of wine and gulped it down. She refilled the glass and lifted it towards the sky.

"This one's for you, Vince. I was such a fool for not appreciating you these last few years. I regret it now, baby. I love you and always will. Please forgive me."

CHAPTER TWENTY-FOUR

"I promise that I won't hit on you, try to kiss you or feel you up. We'll just enjoy a nice dinner after work, some light conversation, and a hand shake to seal our friendship. It's all going to be completely innocent, I promise," Nathan cooed in the sweetest voice he could muster.

Amanda looked at him suspiciously, "No funny stuff, huh? Just an innocent dinner," she asked as she moved back to her desk and gracefully sat down.

"No funny stuff, I mean, not from me. Now if you want to jump my bones, who am I to stop you? But I can assure you, I won't be making any advances," Nathan said with a wink. Laughing at his silliness, Amanda heard herself accept his invitation. A good meal and change of scenery would serve her well. Rozalla's situation had been stressful for all of them. Now that her body was healed and she was returning to life as usual, it gave Amanda and her girl's permission to return to their lives as well.

"Cool! So before I break out into my happy dance, I'm going to return to my office so that I can wrap up a few things. I'll pick you up here at five o'clock sharp," Nathan sang.

"No!" Amanda blurted out.

"But I thought you just said yes?"

"I did, I mean no to your meeting me in here and us walking out together. You know how I feel about giving these office gossips something to talk about. I'll meet you in the garage instead."

"Fair enough." Nathan turned and walked out of Amanda's office with a smile on his face.

She riffled through papers, looked over medical claims, and constantly checked her watch. The time was passing so slowly, 5:00 could not come fast enough. Amanda was finally ready to admit to herself that, despite his height, she was incredibly attracted to Nathan. He was smart, fine, witty, considerate, and she was sure that there were pleasantries to discover about him. Amanda had never allowed herself to consider dating someone from work. Her motto was, "don't shit where you eat." Office affairs could get messy and she wasn't willing to risk her livelihood for the affection of a man. At least not until now. She missed the touch of a man's hands against her skin. She missed being in the throes of passion. And while other men appreciated her odd beauty, Nathan seemed the most genuine.

Arizona's was busy, but thankfully not packed. Amanda hadn't had the delicious food offerings from the dimly lit and well-appointed restaurant in quite a while. The hostess escorted Nathan and Amanda to a nice, cozy booth. Over drinks, they started to share more about their lives with one another.

"So, your sister that was involved with that crazy Harrison, is she your only sibling?" Amanda questioned.

"I'm actually one of four children and the only boy, I might add."

"Oh gracious, that means you're spoiled as hell. A rotten little boy sheltered by his mom and sisters," Amanda said jokingly, although she feared it was the truth.

"Ha! Not at all. My pops wasn't having any of that. He believed that a boy should act like a boy, rough and tumble. He taught me how to be a gentleman, but not soft. I was free to express myself, but if I cried, it had better to have been for good reason."

Amanda breathed a slight sigh of relief as the waitress approached the table to take their order. Nathan ordered a steak and Amanda ordered grilled salmon. Once the waitress walked away, Amanda turned her attention back to her date. "I can't tell you how good it is to hear that you weren't some coddled, snotty-nosed brat. Nothing worse than a grown man with the mentality and behavior of a kid."

"I hear you and I can assure you that is not and never was the case with me. Now please tell me a little bit about your family life. Any siblings or are you daddy's spoiled little princess?" Nathan joked.

"As a matter of fact, I am. I'm sort of an only child. My father had another daughter years before he married my mom. She's much older than I am; we never lived in the same city, which meant we rarely saw one another. So essentially, I grew up as an only child and yes, I was a tad spoiled. But I was also taught the value of a dollar and the importance of hard work and dedication."

"Humph, so that explains why you march around the office like a tyrant," Nathan joked.

"Very funny," Amanda replied with a chuckle. They continued to talk and laugh long after their meals were finished. As the time passed, Amanda found herself attracted to Nathan even more. But soon she realized that it was nine o'clock, and they both had to be at work in the morning. "All right, Mr. Bishop, we'd better get out of here. Are you okay to drive me back to my car?"

Nathan gave her a crazy look, "Woman please! One alcoholic beverage two hours ago does not make Nathan a drunk driver. Now come on sexy, let's go."

The ride back to the garage was filled with music and more light-hearted conversation. Amanda loved that Nathan was ambitious with plans to move up the ranks at work. He earned a good living now, but if he stuck with his plan, his income would eventually sky rocket. Amanda thought to herself, *Funny, ambitious, witty, fine and he smells good. Is he too good to be true?*

CHAPTER TWENTY-FIVE

Aside from the meeting with Detective Bane, Rozalla was excited for the day. Lisa didn't have classes, Carmen was coming up from Athens, and Amanda had decided to take the day off and spend it with the three of them. They all hadn't had a chance to hang out and do something enjoyable since Rozalla had recovered from the whole Harrison fiasco. The only one missing would be Heather, but Rozalla resigned herself to the fact that everyone was right about Heather. She wasn't the kind of friend that Rozalla needed in her life. If only she'd figured that out sooner, things could be so different for her. She'd still have her husband, the man that loved her and always had her best interest at heart.

Rozalla thought back to when she was pregnant with each of her girls. From the moment they found out they were expecting, Vince began to express his love for both Rozalla and their unborn children in the sweetest ways. Rozalla received a small trinket every week as a show of his appreciation for her carrying his child. Chocolates, flowers, gift certificates for massages, always something to show his love. What Rozalla loved most was when he'd lay beside her and rub her belly. He'd talk to the girls, tell them how much he loved them and couldn't wait to meet them. He'd purchased classical music tapes for Rozalla to listen to; Beethoven for Carmen and Chopin for Lisa. He said that he wanted his babies to be born into an environment filled with love and peace. He loved Rozalla and the babies she carried, and the music provided an atmosphere of peace and tranquility. She thought back to how he waited on her hand and foot after she'd given birth. Rozalla laughed at the memories of Vince pushing the girls on the swings, and winning prizes for them every year at the state fair. She also remembered how he used to kiss her, caress her, and make love to her like she was the most beautiful woman on earth.

Rozalla shook her head and wondered how she could have been so stupid and greedy. How could she, as a grown woman, have allowed herself to be so easily influenced by someone that had no idea what real relationships were made of. Heather concentrated on the material, but completely forgot about the love, security, and comfort of a real man. True enough, Rozalla allowed Heather to get in her head and screw with her way of thinking, but Rozalla knew that ultimately this was all her fault. Her greedy ways and mean spirit were what took her husband away from her. The doorbell rang, snatching Rozalla from her thoughts. She wiped the tears from her eyes and padded off towards the door.

"Are you okay, honey?" Amanda asked as she glided through the door. "You look like you've been crying."

"Ignore me, girl. I just got caught up in memories," Rozalla chuckled uneasily.

Amanda walked to the kitchen with her friend. "Got Vince on your mind?"

"Of course. I can't help but remember what an amazing man he was, how much he loved me and the girls. Realizing how my stupidity and greed took him away."

"Don't be so hard on yourself, Roz. Daily stress or a number of other things could have caused his heart attack. Yes, he loved you all with his whole heart, but remember, he'd never want you to be miserable. Vince would want you to move on with your life in a positive manner. You've learned a hard lesson, and now you know what not to do next time."

"What's happening next time?" Lisa quizzed as she and Carmen walked into the kitchen, interrupting Rozalla and Amanda's conversation.

"Nothing, my nosey little girl. I didn't hear y'all come in; let me grab my purse and we can head out." Rozalla disappeared to her room and reappeared with an envelope full of papers and her handbag. "Who's driving?"

"I'll do the honors," Amanda volunteered. "I'm so hungry, and I feel like if I drive, I'll eat sooner."

"Cool your heels, missy. Remember, we have to go by the police station first," Rozalla reminded her.

"Humph, I forgot about that. Well, let's get a move on because there's a steak at Houston's with my name on it."

Fortunately, the ride to the police station only took about twenty minutes. It was Amanda's hope that this little meeting wouldn't take long either. She felt like the longer it dragged on, the more opportunity it would give Rozalla to fall back into a depression over everything she'd been through.

"Come on back, ladies, I promise not to keep you all too long," said Detective Bane as he escorted them to a small conference room. "Can I get you all anything to drink?"

"No thank you," sang out from each woman.

"So, what have you found out about Harrison's whereabouts, Detective?" Rozalla asked, trying to cut to the point.

"We've been closely watching an account that we found linked to him. Now we don't think that he has returned to town, but someone removed the money from the account for him. We requested the bank records and found that someone named Heather Ramos was a signer on the account and has pulled out every dime."

"Heather! You've got to be mistaken, Detective. Heather is a friend of mine, she would never betray me by hooking up with Harrison. She knows what that man put me through," Rozalla cried.

"I'm sorry, Ms. Harper, but we are positive that it's her. We were hoping to track her down at work, but apparently she resigned a few days ago. No notice or anything, she just took off."

"So they got cash advances on the two fraudulent credit accounts and ran off into the sunset? How far do they think they're going to get on less than fifty grand?" Rozalla was devastated and confused. How could her so called friend had done this to her.

"Ms. Harper, it appears that she withdrew close to four-hundred thousand dollars. That's plenty to run off and start a new life with. Or at least enough to tide them over until Harrison comes up with his next scheme."

"Mama, are you sure that you only found two fraudulent accounts? Could there have been more?" Carmen asked as gently as she could.

"I'm sure. I checked all of the mail and didn't find anything else. I checked all of my credit cards and aside from the charges that Harrison made in Hawaii, they were all in order." Rozalla dropped her head on the desk and wept. "How could I have been so stupid? How could Heather have been so evil? I mean damn, is she that desperate for love?"

Amanda tried her best to comfort Rozalla, but she knew that little of what she said or did at this point would matter. Carmen and Lisa sat there, also wondering how their mother could have been so gullible, so stupid. She had a perfectly good life and didn't appreciate it, didn't value and honor their father as she should have. *What a hard lesson to learn*, they thought, but thankfully, neither verbalized their disgust.

"Other than bank cards and the money you gave him to invest, are you sure that Harrison didn't have access to anything else?" Amanda asked as she rubbed Rozalla's back, hoping to comfort her.

"I checked my checking account and it's in tact, as well as my savings account. But I don't keep a bunch of money in them anyway. The bulk of my funds are in an investment account that Vince had opened years ago. Thankfully, I put the life insurance money in it as well."

"Well that's good to hear," chimed Detective Bane. "But I would still advise you to keep an eye on all of your accounts. But rest assured, we're still working diligently to track him down. This information you gave me today will add to the charges once we get him in custody."

The ladies pilled back into the car and headed for the restaurant. This time, the ride seemed to take forever and it was eerily quiet. There wasn't any real conversation taking place across the table, while they waited for their meals to be served. Once the food did come, Rozalla barely ate a bite. Instead, she mindlessly moved the food around on her plate. A little while later, the waitress approached the table and asked if anyone was interested in dessert. The answer was a resounding no. They all wanted to get out of there, especially Rozalla. She could feel her girls and Amanda looking at her with a mixture of disgust and pity.

"I know what you all are thinking, so you may as well go ahead and say it. Tell me how stupid I am, how desperate I must have looked. Tell me how Harrison probably picked me out of the crowd as an easy target. Tell me that I'm getting exactly what I deserve," Rozalla sniffled.

"No one was thinking that, Mama," Carmen gently said.

"Yes, I was. I'll be the honest one, and tell you that I was in fact thinking that," Lisa blurted out. "I was also thinking that after Heather saw how easily influenced you were, she decided to join Harrison's gravy train when the opportunity presented itself."

"That's enough, Lisa. Now is not the time."

"Then when is the right time, Amanda? When should we speak the truth? Maybe if we'd been more vocal in the beginning, none of this would have happened." Lisa pulled no punches with her words.

Carmen shot her sister an evil look. "Why don't you shut the hell up, Lisa, and try to remember how harshly vocal you were back then as well. It was probably your mean-spirited words that further pushed Mama into the arms of that jackass."

"That's right, blame the only one in this damn car brave enough to speak the truth," Lisa huffed.

The car grew silent again. All that could be heard were the sniffles coming from Rozalla, as she unsuccessfully tried to silence her crying. Once they pulled up to the house, Lisa jumped out and marched towards the house. She ignored Carmen calling out to her with suggestions that she leave. They all filed into the house and Amanda didn't hesitate to pop open a bottle of wine. She needed to calm her nerves and thought that a drink would help calm Rozalla's nerves as well. When she passed Rozalla the wine, the glass almost hit the floor. Instead of holding her hand out to take the glass, Rozalla had jumped up and sprinted out of the room.

"Where are you going?" Amanda yelled out behind her.

Rozalla dashed into her bedroom and hastily opened the lockbox that she kept all of her important papers in. She was confident that Harrison had not gained access to her investment account, but with all that had happened, she wanted to confirm that the money Vince had left for them was safe. She flipped through the paper, picked up the phone, and called the bank to check the balance. If all was as it should be, she'd have close to $400,000 safely sitting and collecting interest.

"Thank you for calling SunTrust Bank. This is Avery, how may I help you?"

"Hi Avery, I need to check the balance on my account please?"

"Of course, may I have the account number please?"

"Yes, it's 456-789-123."

"Thank you. Please verify your name, address, and the last four digits of your social?"

Rozalla recited the information to the customer service representative and waited for her balance. The thirty seconds it took Avery to relay the information seemed like an eternity. When she came back to the phone and stated, "Ms. Harper, you have a balance of $226.15," Rozalla collapsed to the floor and screamed like a wounded animal.

CHAPTER TWENTY-SIX

"Oh God, oh God, what have I done!" Rozalla cried and screamed. "I'm sorry, I'm so sorry. Please help me, God. Everything Vince worked and died for is gone, I ruined it all. I destroyed the only man that ever loved me and ruined everything. I'm so sorry, Vince! I'm sorry, I'm so sorry," she screamed.

Vince sat on the side of the bed, looking at his wife, and wondering what was tormenting her. But as her screams grew more mournful and painful, he decided it was time to take her out of her misery. He reached over and shook her.

"Roz, wake up, baby. Wake up," he said gently. When that didn't work, he spoke louder and shook her more vigorously. "Roz, wake up!"

Rozalla jumped and sat straight up in the bed, barely able to catch her breath. She looked at Vince and wasn't sure what to think. Was she dreaming, had he come back to comfort her? It was the expression on his face that let her know that this was real, and he'd just awakened her from a nightmare.

"What in the world were you dreaming about?"

Rozalla leapt across the bed and flung herself around Vince's neck. "Babe, I have never been so glad to see you. I love you, Vince, I love you!"

Vince barely returned her embrace. He didn't care to hear how much she loved him because her behavior had told him more than her words ever could.

"Babe, I'm so sorry for saying those ugly things to you. I didn't mean them and now I realize how ungrateful I've been," Rozalla confessed. She sat back on the bed, looked her husband in the face and told him about her horrible nightmare. She told him how she'd dreamed that he died and all that transpired after his passing. Even though it was all a dream, she was still ashamed to tell him of her behavior and stupidity.

Vince looked at her, unmoved by her words or tears. "You may have had a bad dream, Roz, but what was very real was how you told me that I could drop dead. Do you know how hurtful it is for your spouse to tell you that your death would bring them joy? All I've ever done is try to make you happy and up until a few years ago, I thought we'd built a good life together. I've tried to give you everything you wanted, but it was never enough. You were never satisfied. I took your verbal abuse and that stank attitude of yours, and in spite of it, I still loved you and tried to make you happy. But I can't do it anymore, Roz, I deserve better."

"And I'm going to be better, babe. I'm going to give you better. I swear Vince, I will be the woman that you fell in love with. I'll be the loyal and devoted wife that I was before. We'll forget these past four years and go back to how we used to be. I'll be so good to you and I swear I'll never hurt you again."

"I know you'll never hurt me again, Roz, because you won't have the opportunity. I want a divorce," Vince announced as he stood up, grabbed his packed bag and walked out.

Rozalla was in shock. She couldn't believe that Vince was actually going to leave her. She couldn't let that happen, she wouldn't just let him leave without a fight. She jumped off the bed and ran after him. She never imagined she'd be the kind of woman that would throw herself at the feet of any man. But there she was, running behind her husband and literally wrapping her arms around his legs. All self-respect was out the window as she cried on her knees. "Please Vince, please don't leave me. I swear I'll be a better wife," she promised.

The commotion woke Lisa and lured her from her bedroom. She was shocked to see her mother on the floor begging like some stray dog, and more shocked that her father would allow it. "What in the world is going on in here?"

"Lisa, please come and get your mother. I need to go and this entire situation has gotten completely out of hand," Vince huffed. He was clearly unmoved by Rozalla and her sudden show of desperation. He'd never asked her to beg, all he'd wanted was her love and respect. He wanted the closeness that they once shared, her appreciation and admiration. Vince simply wanted a little reciprocity.

"What has gotten out of hand? Mama, why in the world are you on the floor begging at his feet?" Lisa was lost in a state of confusion.

"Tell her, Vince. Tell your daughter that you're leaving us," Rozalla cried.

"I'm not leaving y'all, Rozalla, I'm leaving you," Vince clarified.

"What do you mean you're leaving, Daddy? Where are you going?" Lisa's voice became more high pitched with every question.

Vince put his bag down, bent over and lifted Rozalla to her feet. He led both his wife and daughter to the sofa. "Look, let's all calm down. Lisa, you know I love you guys so much, but your mom and I have hit a major road block. We've got some things to deal with, and while we do so, I've decided to stay elsewhere."

"I know I've messed up, babe. I know I've taken you for granted and treated you poorly. I apologize for everything I've done wrong, and I know that I don't have a right to ask you for anything, but please give me an opportunity to make things right. Please, Vince, let's just start over?" Rozalla whimpered with puppy dog eyes.

Lisa listened to her mother plead her case, but she didn't dare voice an opinion. The truth was, she completely understood why her father wanted to leave, and honestly wondered what took him so long. He'd given Rozalla everything he had, but she'd made it clear that his love wasn't good enough and neither were his material goods. Rozalla always wanted more and pushed him away when he didn't provide it. Lisa couldn't think of anyone that would voluntarily stick around for the mistreatment that she'd dished out. She wrapped her arms around her mom and rocked her gently. Lisa wiped Rozalla's tears and told her it would all be okay. As she consoled her mama, she looked up and gave her father a look of understanding. Although she could sympathize with him, it didn't stop the silent tears from falling as she watched him walk out the door.

CHAPTER TWENTY-SEVEN

Vince had landed on the doorstep of his longtime friend and confidant, Scottie Ross. He and Scottie had been close since third grade. Scottie had just relocated to the Atlanta area with his grandparents, after he'd loss his parents to a house fire. Vince ran next door to introduce himself to the little boy that, as his mother put it, had lived through an unspeakable tragedy. Vince remembered his mother telling him to be nice to the new little boy. She said that he wouldn't have any friends and she was appointing Vince the boy's designated buddy. "Introduce him to your other friends, son. Let him know that he's got a friend in you," she'd instructed. Vince took his mother's words to heart and the boys had formed an unbreakable friendship.

Before Vince could even ring the doorbell, Scottie swung the door open, stepped aside and allowed Vince to enter. "Come on in, man."

"Thanks bruh, I appreciate you letting me crash for a bit."

"Mi casa su casa. You're welcome to stay as long as you like. Besides, if it weren't for you I wouldn't have this place," Scottie admitted as he looked around at his small, nicely appointed house.

"C'mon man, you did this all on your own. All I did was provide a reference; you're the one that locked down that good job, paid off all that debt, and actually saved your money. And I know that was no easy task for Mr. Spend-A-Lot," Vince joked.

Everyone that knew Scottie knew that he didn't believe in saving money. His motto was, "You can't take it with you." Then he met his girlfriend, Haley, and everything changed.

She was a therapist with a successful practice. Scottie couldn't believe that someone like her would actually give him the time of day. However, their chance encounter at Starbucks proved him wrong. He was the most handsome man she'd ever seen. His mocha complexion and hazel eyes immediately attracted her. Scottie's slender, but muscular body made her tingle. But that million-dollar smile of his convinced Haley to speak up and introduce herself. Their first date had turned into six years of love and devotion. In the beginning, she'd refused to go over to his ratty apartment or ride in his 1987 El Camino that had duct tape securing the steering column. Instead, she talked to him about building his credit, advancing his career and working towards owning his own property. He followed her advice, turned to Vince for a little help, and eventually, all the pieces had fallen into place.

"Is Haley cool with me staying for a while?" Vince asked.

"Man please, this is my house. It doesn't matter if she's cool with it or not."

"Humph, so she said it was cool, huh?"

"Yeah, she's cool with it," Scottie chuckled. "She was actually going to be spending a little more time at her own place anyway. Her little cousin is staying with her for a couple of months, and she wants to spend as much time with her as possible."

"Cool. Where should I throw this bag?"

"Take it on back to the guest room. I'm going to grab a beer from the fridge while you do that, do you want one?" Scottie offered.

"It's a little early to be drinking isn't it?"

"It's five o'clock somewhere."

"You've got a point," Vince declared. "And after the morning I've had, I could use a cold one to settle my nerves." He took his bag to the back room and dropped it on the floor. Vince plopped down on the edge of the bed with his head in his hands, wondering how things got to this point. He never imagined that there would be a breakdown in his and Rozalla's marriage. However, he refused to let her continue with her ungrateful attitude and disrespectful mouth. That foolishness was not what he'd signed up for.

"You all right back there?" Scottie called out.

"Yeah, I'll be up in a second and that beer better be cold."

The guys sat around talking about all that had transpired between Vince and Rozalla earlier in the day. Vince thought it was ridiculous that a dream could be the cause of Rozalla wanting to change her evil ways. Quite honestly, he thought it was just some kind of silly ploy to keep him from leaving. He surmised that she must have overheard the phone call he'd made around 2:00 a.m. The call where he told Scottie that he'd decided to leave her. Vince was convinced that she'd heard every word, and decided to pull out all the punches to get him to stay. He was done though, and her tricks wouldn't work. Rozalla had mistreated him for the last time.

CHAPTER TWENTY-EIGHT

Amanda had run over to Rozalla's as soon as she'd heard the news. She tried to comfort her friend, tried to reassure her that she'd be able to win her husband back. When Rozalla asked her if her behavior had been bad enough to warrant Vince's leaving, however, she couldn't lie.

"In all honesty, yes, your behavior has been horrible. You've been unappreciative and mean. I don't know what or who inspired this attitude of ungratefulness in you, well actually, I do, but that's another story for another day. The point is, I love you, but you have been unbelievably unkind to your husband." Amanda didn't believe in mincing words when it came to speaking the truth.

"You didn't have to be so blunt about it," Rozalla said flatly.

"Would you rather I sugar-coat it, try to make you feel better about how crappy you've been? Come on, Roz, you know that's not my style. But you also know that I'll do everything in my power to help you two come back together as the couple you were always meant to be."

Rozalla wiped her tears and blew her nose. "Thank you, Amanda, I'd really appreciate that." She sat in silence for a moment while Amanda went to prepare them each a cup of hot tea. Why had she listened to Heather in the first place? The woman tried to be a good friend, but the fact of the matter was that she knew nothing about Rozalla and Vince's marriage. All she knew about was the complaining Rozalla did at work, which was usually over trivial things. Heather didn't know how hard Vince worked to support his family, or how he'd do anything to ensure the happiness and success of their girls. She didn't know about the hot baths, and good meals that Vince would prepare for her after she'd had a long, hard day at the hospital. She wasn't aware of the love they'd make in the midnight hour. The way Vince lovingly touched her skin, caressed her breasts, licked, and sucked her to ecstasy before entering, and stroking the very soul of her. Rozalla's body tingled at the very thought of it.

"Be careful, it's hot," Amanda warned, snatching Rozalla from her trip down memory lane. "You look a million miles away, where'd you go?"

"Just thinking about how I let Heather screw everything up for me."

"Rozalla, Heather didn't screw things up for you. You did that all on your own. Yes, she planted seeds in your head, but you're a grown, forty-three year old woman. You knew that she wasn't correct in the crap she was saying, but you never bothered to correct her." With each of her words, Amanda made her friend cry a little bit harder. "I'm sorry, Rozalla, I didn't mean to come down on you so hard. Please forgive me."

"Forgive you for speaking the truth? No forgiveness necessary."

Amanda decided to try and lighten the mood with a confession. "So as tragic as your dream was, there's actually a funny truth to it."

"And what in the hell could that be?" Rozalla asked.

"I finally caved to Nathan's silly advances and went out on a date with him."

"Are you serious?" Rozalla asked with big grin on her face. "I knew it would finally happen. Tell me everything."

Amanda was all too happy to share the details of the beautiful evening she'd had with Nathan. He'd been a complete gentleman. They enjoyed a good meal and great music at Sweet Georgia's Juke Joint, and the goodnight kiss was proof that they had great chemistry. "We're going to Café Intermezzo for coffee and dessert after work on Friday. I know I'll see him at work, but I'm really excited about our next date."

"I have a great idea! How about Vince and I join you guys? Maybe if I ask him out on a date, it'll open the door for us to begin our reconciliation. Being around new love always seems to reignite the spark in old love."

"Now that's a great idea."

~~~

Devastated by Vince's harsh and emotionless rejection of the date invitation, Rozalla headed for the hospital with tears streaming down her face. She knew that he was angry and hurt, but she was sure that a few days away from her would've given him a new perspective on things.

Sadly, that had not happened. Instead of missing her, he seemed to be growing angrier with her, and only desired to increase the distance between them. Rozalla had urged her daughters to talk to their father, to try and convince him to give her another chance. Both of them had declined, saying that she needed to give him a little space to sort things out.

When she'd called Amanda distraught over his rejection, even she had encouraged Rozalla to back off and give Vince some space. In desperation, she went to the hospital to talk to Heather, hoping that she'd be willing to help her win her husband back.

"Rozalla, what's wrong? Nothing has happened to your family, has it?" Heather rushed to Rozalla and ushered her to one of the chairs in her office.

Her body shaking from the tears and the agony of losing Vince, made it almost impossible for her to speak. "Vince left me," she finally managed through tears.

"He left *you*? He's got some damn nerve. All of the crap you've been putting up with from him, with his cheap ass. How dare he?" Heather spat venomously.

"No, how dare I. How dare I treat him so poorly after all he's been to me and done for me? I only told you the annoying things, Heather. I never took the time to explain all the good that Vince has done over the years. I should've given you the whole story and not gotten wrapped up in the material things that I didn't have. Stuff that I never really cared about in the first place," Rozalla explained as she shuttered with regret.

"Fine, maybe you didn't tell me the whole story, but you haven't done anything to warrant his leaving you. I say that if he was so anxious to leave, let his ass go. There are plenty of men out there that would kill to date you."

"I'm asking you for help, Heather. I don't want to let him go, I need my husband back," Rozalla screamed as she jumped up and ran from Heather's office. She heard her friend calling after her, but didn't slow her stride. Distraught, she ran through the hospital and down the stairs to the surgical wing. Two rooms had been prepped for surgery. She picked one, grabbed a scalpel off the tray and laid on the cold, hard table. "I'm doing this for us, Vince. This will bring you back to me," Rozalla said aloud as she took the scalpel and cut across each of her wrists.

Fifteen hours later, Rozalla woke up and saw her daughters, Amanda, and most importantly, Vince, at her bedside. She knew this would bring him back to her. When she raised up to hug him though, she realized that her arms were secured to the bed. Why had they tied her down?

"What's going on? I want to get up. I want to sit up so I can hug you, Vince. Let me up baby."

"Shhh, its okay, Roz. The doctor is on his way in now," Vince replied as he stroked her hair.

"Carmen, tell your dad that it's okay to let me up." When Carmen remained silent, Rozalla became very anxious. "Why are you all looking at me like I'm crazy? Let me up, let me up now!"

The doctor entered the room and advised Rozalla to calm down. "Mrs. Harper, unless you want to be sedated again, you're going to have to calm down. Now as you know, you attempted to take your life. We have to keep you restrained because clearly, you're a danger to yourself. But rest assured, we're going to make sure that you get all the help you need."

"No, I wasn't really going to kill myself," Rozalla explained. "I just wanted to show my husband how far I'd go to get him back. I did this for us, Vince, for you."

Sickened by her words, Vince withdrew his hand from her. "This wasn't the way, Roz. This is not how you fix us. You need help."

"No babe, I don't need help, I just need you. See how you came running to my side? That's proof that you still love me. You love me, Vince."

"Okay, this will calm you, Mrs. Harper and then we're going to transport you to the eighth floor for further evaluation," the doctor explained as he released a clear substance from a needle into her arm.

"No, the eighth floor is for crazy people. I'm not crazy, I just want my husband back. Vince, come back. Please come back and take me home," she begged, but it was all in vain. The last thing she saw before slipping into unconsciousness was her husband turning his back and walking out on her again.

PART II
THE RESSURECTION OF LOVE?

CHAPTER TWENTY-NINE

The past three days had been the longest seventy-two hours of Rozalla's life. When she'd made the rash decision to slit her wrists as a last ditch effort to win her husband back, she'd failed to take the mandatory three-day psychiatric stay into account. Just as she'd planned, Vince came rushing to her side. But when he learned that she'd cut herself just to get him back, he walked out of the hospital without looking back. Rozalla was devastated. But the hospital stay made her realize that it was her greed, selfishness, and ability to be persuaded by others that had destroyed her marriage. As she thought back on how she'd told Vince she'd be happier if he were dead, tears filled her eyes. She wiped the tears away and thought that now was the time for her to clean out her friend closet, rid herself of the ones that, like an ill-fitting sweater, never should've been allowed in her life. It was time to get back to the selfless, caring woman that her husband and daughters knew and loved.

As they wheeled Rozalla through the doors, she watched her real friend, Amanda, pull the car around to the hospital entrance.

"Hey chica, you ready to go home?" she asked as she opened the passenger side door for her best friend.

"It's so completely ridiculous that they made me leave out in a wheelchair," Rozalla whined as she slid into the car. Thanking the hospital attendant as she closed the door, Rozalla watched as Amanda pranced her lean, beautiful self around the car and took her seat behind the wheel.

"Do you mind if we stop and grab a bite to eat before you drop me off? That hospital food was absolutely disgusting."

"I'm pretty hungry myself. I was so busy trying to tie things up at work that I didn't take time to eat lunch. How about some soul food?"

"Amanda, you must've read my mind. Just the thought of Gladys' Chicken and Waffles has my mouth watering."

They rode for the next few blocks in silence. Rozalla was reflecting on all of her bad decisions and Amanda wondered what she could and could not discuss with her friend. She wasn't sure how fragile Rozalla's mental state was and didn't want to say anything to send her spiraling out of control. She glanced out the corner of her eye and saw Rozalla gazing at the thin incisions on her wrists.

"In a couple of months no one will even be able to see them," Amanda assured.

Rozalla looked out the window as they passed by the Fox Theater and saw the marquee announcing the return of her favorite dance troop. Joyful memories flooded her mind. "Oh, the Alvin Ailey Dance Theater is in town. Did you know that Vince has taken me to that show every year for the past ten years?"

"I remember. It always coincides with you all's anniversary," Amanda blurted out and immediately regretted her comment. Fortunately, Rozalla gave her a half smile and pulled her sleeves back over the scars on her wrists.

"You don't have to tip-toe around me, Amanda, or watch everything that you say. I'm still the same Rozalla you've always known. I just made an incredibly stupid decision. But please don't censor yourself of start treating me differently."

"I'm so glad you said that. I was going crazy trying to figure out what I could and couldn't say and how delicate I was going to have to be with you," Amanda confessed as she whipped her car into the small parking lot behind the restaurant.

They were greeted by the hostess and immediately seated. Rozalla and Amanda perused the menu in silence. Rozalla was quiet because she was so embarrassed by her behavior and thought that every word that escaped her lips would be harshly judged. Yes, Amanda was her oldest and dearest friend, but she was also very level headed and judgmental of those that didn't always operate from a place of common sense. But the silence was maddening. It wasn't the comfortable silence that sometimes settled between them. This was a heavy, thick cloud of silence that made them both uncomfortable.

"Please Amanda, just say whatever you need to in order for us to get past this. I asked you to not tip-toe around me and I meant it. I swear, this silence is worse than anything you could say."

The waitress came and took their drink order, told them about the day's specials, and asked if they had any questions. Amanda politely asked her to give them a few minutes before she returned with their drinks or asked for their food order.

"Rozalla, I'm trying really hard to understand how you thought that this stunt would bring Vince back to you. For the last couple of years you seemed to have lost your natural mind. You waited until you were in your forties before you fell under the spell of peer pressure. Who does that? Vince is the kind of man that women look for their whole lives and you had him. You had a man that tried to give you the world, that loved you unconditionally and after twenty-three years of marriage, that suddenly wasn't good enough for you. You trusted some stupid ass tramp to tell you what you should have instead of being thankful for all that you had." Amanda had to stop and catch herself. She hadn't meant to get so angry or raise her voice, but the frustration she felt with Rozalla was all consuming.

Angry with her friend, but mostly with herself, Rozalla banged her fist on the table. "You don't think that I realize this now? Don't you think that all I've done for the last three days is think about how stupid I've been? And to think, it took a damn nightmare for me to realize all the mistakes that I've made. My question to you is why didn't you say all of this before? Why did you wait until I crashed and burned before you spoke up?"

"Excuse me! I told you two years ago that I thought Heather Ramos was trouble. I told you that she didn't seem like the kind of woman that would rejoice in your happiness. But you told me that I was jealous of your new found friendship. You let her influence you and convince you that what Vince offered was no longer good enough. Vince himself told you that he didn't care for her. So don't try to place the blame for your foolishness at my feet. You need to take full responsibility for the mess that you're in," Amanda fussed and pointed like she was a mother scolding her child.

Rozalla no longer tried to contain her emotions. She sat at the table and sobbed like a baby. "You're right, I've been a complete idiot. My daughters must think I'm a fool. When they left the hospital that first day, they didn't even come back to check on me. They didn't call or anything. Not only have I damaged my relationship with Vince, but with my girls as well. But how do I fix it, Amanda? How do I repair all the damage I've done?"

CHAPTER THIRTY

Vince retreated to the small guest room at his buddy, Scottie's house. Sitting on the side of the bed with his head in his hands, he hadn't been able to get Rozalla off of his mind. He wondered if she'd made it home from the hospital. Had she gotten her mind right and figured out how to move on without him? And while he wondered that about her, he had to admit that he hadn't quite figured it out for himself. Rozalla and their girls had been his life, the reason he lived and worked the way that he had. With the girls grown, this was supposed to be the time for him and Rozalla to travel and try new things. They were supposed to be enjoying their empty nest, but Rozalla had completely ruined everything and growing old together was no longer an option. The knock at his door snatched Vince from his thoughts. He jumped up to open the door, figuring it was Scottie. To his surprise, his daughters, Carmen and Lisa were on the other side.

"Hi Daddy," Carmen sang while Lisa threw her arms around his neck.

"What a pleasant surprise. To what do I owe this pleasure?" Vince smiled as he hugged his girls.

"We were hoping to drag you away for a bit," admitted Lisa. "Mom is home and we thought that maybe you'd want to grab some lunch with us and then swing by and see her. What do you say?"

Vince smiled and motioned for the girls to walk back up the short hallway. "Let's go to the living room and talk," he instructed.

Once they'd all taken a seat, he began to explain why he had no intention of going to see his wife.

"Your mom has made some wild choices lately that I can't begin to understand. However, I do understand that she needs time to get her mind right and reevaluate all the foolish decisions she's made. Unfortunately, while she sorts it all out I cannot be around. I won't be a part of this crazy life she's chosen to lead. I love your mom, but I'm tired. I'm tired of the complaining, the unreasonable financial demands, and all of her demeaning insults. I wish her well, but I don't want anything to do with her."

"I completely understand how you feel. We feel the same way. But you can't lose sight of the fact that we're a family, Daddy," said Lisa.

"Girls, in my mind the three of us are family. I'm not anything to your mom, now and I plan to see an attorney soon and file for divorce."

"Daddy no," cried Carmen. She tried to catch all the tears as they rolled down her face, but it was useless. She looked to Lisa in hopes that she'd join her in an emotional plea. But to her dismay Lisa sat dry eyed and stern faced. "Lisa say something."

"I'm sorry, Carmen, but I don't blame him. I think they both need time to sort things out."

"Thank you, baby girl for understanding," Vince said as he patted Lisa on the hand. He then turned his attention to his eldest daughter, Carmen. "I know that this is difficult for you and for that I'm sorry. But my heart just can't take the abuse anymore. And I really think you need to go talk to your mom because she likely feels the same as me. We both need to rethink everything."

Taking their father's advice, Carmen and Lisa finished the drinks they'd stopped to have at a neighborhood bar and headed to their mother's house. They wanted to see if she was in fact wanting to reevaluate her marriage or if she desperately wanted her husband back. Carmen maneuvered the car through afternoon traffic and bobbed her head to the music that boomed from the car speakers. Lisa reached over and turned the music down. Carmen always played her radio too loudly and Lisa hated shouting over it.

"Carmen, now that we've found out what Dad's mindset is, have you prepared yourself to hear the same thing from Mama? I know she said that she wanted him back, but that was when she first slit her wrists. Since that stupid attempt failed, she may have changed her mind. You know how unpredictable she's become."

"Hell, I guess I'm ready for anything now, Lisa. I never in a million years would've imagined any of this happening, but now I realize that anything is possible. Even the most ridiculous shit."

Carmen turned the radio back up and sang along to the hot new song by Adele. Lisa decided to tolerate the volume and allow herself to get lost in the music. As they turned down the tree lined street, both of the women were pleased to see Amanda back over at their mom's house. She'd been spending a great deal of time with Rozalla and they were thankful for it. Neither of them had been able to put their anger over her suicide attempt behind them long enough to spend any real time with her.

"You ready?"

"Yeah girl, let's go on in here and see where Mama's head is," Carmen replied.

Lisa knocked on the door a couple of times and then used her key to get in. As she opened the door, she was greeted by Amanda who was walking briskly in the direction of the front door.

"Well hello ladies. Isn't this a nice surprise? Come on in the kitchen, your mom is back here cooking up some salmon croquettes and her famous hash brown potatoes."

"Umm, it does smell good," confessed Carmen as they walked through the house. She couldn't help reminiscing on the days when Rozalla cooked for them and the joyful conversations that flowed as they enjoyed her gourmet meals. But as soon as she laid eyes on her mom, the fond memories disappeared.

Rozalla looked up to see who was accompanying Amanda through the door. Her expression was clearly not one of joy when she realized it was her girls.

"Well look who the cat drug in, Judas and her sidekick, Betrayal."

"Really Mama? That's how you're going to greet us?" Lisa asked with furred brows.

"Mama, we just came to check on you and see how you're doing. We should talk a couple of things out," Carmen said as she tried to ease the tension that was building. "I promise that we didn't come here for a fight."

Rozalla eased her expression. "Well I've got enough food here for all of us, so pull up a chair, fill a plate and we'll talk while we eat."

Her daughters did as they were instructed, but they didn't immediately start talking. Instead they enjoyed the potatoes that were laced with red and green peppers, onions, garlic, and cayenne pepper. The salmon was lightly fried with chopped onions and topped with a caramelized peach glaze and was equally as fabulous. They'd always admired how Rozalla could take an ordinary meal and make it extraordinary. And they couldn't help but think of how much their father would enjoy this meal. It was one of his favorites, the one he requested most often.

"So Carmen, what brings you and your sister by?" Amanda asked. She figured she'd may as well open the door for the conversation that they all obviously had to have.

When Carmen didn't speak up fast enough for her liking, Lisa jumped in with both feet. "We were wondering how you felt about Daddy. Now that you've had time to get yourself together and recover from your little incident, we wondered if your perspective had changed. Do you still want to be with Daddy or are you ready to move on and start a life without him?"

"Before I answer that question, let me pose one to you two. Why did you abandon me when I needed you most? I realize that what I did was stupid and desperate. I also realize that the way I'd been treating your father was reprehensible, but not once did I mistreat either of you or stop being the loving mother I'd always been. So please help me understand why it was so easy for y'all to walk out of that hospital and not look back?"

Stunned by her question, neither Carmen nor Lisa had an immediate answer for her. It was true that she'd treated Vince poorly and they hated the way she made him feel, but she never treated them with anything but love. Finally, Lisa managed to formulate a sensible, honest answer. "Mama, I guess I got really caught up in the way you were treating Daddy. I've always known that you loved me, but to see you turn on him like that was maddening. Day in and day out I was there to hear you scream and holler about how he needed to do more, be more, give more. You spoke to him like he was some bum on the street. Seeing you mistreat him made it hard for me to not become angry and disgusted with you."

"And you have to admit, that whole suicide attempt was a little insane. Not only had you put Daddy through the ringer, but then you decided to play head games with all of us," Carmen chimed in. "The way you cut your wrists let us all know that you had no intention of dying. Mama, the emotional manipulation of it was too much."

Rozalla sat with tears streaming down her face. She knew that her treatment of Vince had been horrific. She threw all the years he'd spent loving and providing for her back in his face like it was nothing. She was ashamed of herself.

"Both of you are right, I treated him terribly and tried to scare him back to my side. For that I am truly sorry, but as my children you still shouldn't have turned your back on me."

"Maybe you're right, Mama, but we're here now. Speaking for myself, I have no intention of disconnecting from you like that again. I'm sorry," Carmen said as she reached out and took her mom's hand.

"Yeah, I'm here with you now, Mama. And more than anything, I want to see us all back together as a family. But what do you want?" Lisa asked.

Rozalla wiped the tears from her cheeks. "I want my husband back. When I asked y'all to help me talk with him and you said to give him time, it was like you plunged a knife in my heart. I realize now that he may need some time, but my feelings haven't changed. I love that man and I want him back. I want the opportunity to make up for all the wrong I've done, for my mistreatment of him. I want the chance to make him happy again. But I guess the bigger question is what does he want? Has he even asked about me?"

The girls glanced at each other, neither wanting to tell her about Vince's plans for a divorce.

"Just tell me," Rozalla pleaded.

Lisa looked at her with loving eyes. "Sorry Mama, but he still says he wants a divorce. He says his heart can't take any more of the abuse."

Rozalla took a deep breath and smiled. "That's what he thinks he wants and I understand why. But if that man thinks he's divorcing me then he's got another thought coming. Before the deal is done, he will be back in this house with me. This is where he belongs."

said to give him time, it was like you plunged a knife in my heart. I realize now that he may need some time, but my feelings haven't changed. I love that man and I want him back. I want the opportunity to make up for all the wrong I've done, for my mistreatment of him. I want the chance to make him happy again. But I guess the bigger question is what does he want? Has he even asked about me?"

The girls glanced at each other, neither wanting to tell her about Vince's plans for a divorce.

"Just tell me," Rozalla pleaded.

Lisa looked at her with loving eyes. "Sorry Mama, but he still says he wants a divorce. He says his heart can't take any more of the abuse."

Rozalla took a deep breath and smiled. "That's what he thinks he wants and I understand why. But if that man thinks he's divorcing me then he's got another thought coming. Before the deal is done, he will be back in this house with me. This is where he belongs."

"Then maybe there is something we can do about it," Haley said with a wicked grin on her face.

"Oh hell, I know that look. What crazy idea do you have rolling around in that beautiful, blonde head of yours?"

"Don't say it like that, my chocolate delight, it's a great idea. We're going to take Vince out on a double date. Pauletta is one of the other therapists in the practice. She's beautiful, but she knows how to turn on the crazy. Maybe a date with her will help him see that no one is perfect and no one will be able to take the place of Rozalla. We did this fake double date thing with one of her friends and it worked like a charm. I turned on the crazy and her friend went running back to his spouse. Pauletta will be glad to return the favor and like I said, she knows how to turn on the crazy."

"Babe, that sounds a little unethical."

"Scottie, we would never do this with our patients, but our friends are fair game."

Finally conceding, Scottie asked, "Fine, can you set it up for tomorrow?"

"Consider it done," Haley snickered as she grabbed her iPhone.

When the couple heard Vince moving around in the kitchen, they knew this was their opportunity to pose the idea of a double date. They walked in the kitchen and the foolish look on their faces alerted Vince that they had something up their sleeves.

"No, I haven't seen Rozalla and I have no plans to see her. Yes, we spoke briefly. Just long enough for me to ask her to leave my mail out where I could find it. The silly look on your faces lets me know that you're up to something, but if it has anything to do with Roz, then keep it to yourselves," Vince advised.

"Actually, Mr. Know It All, I wanted to invite you out on a double date with us," Haley said with a smirk. "I'm done trying to get you to talk to Rozalla. I realize that you want to be done with that relationship so this is the perfect opportunity to dip your toe back into the dating pool."

Vince looked at her suspiciously. "Is this one of your little therapy head games?"

"No, not at all. Vince all you do is work, come home and watch television until you fall asleep. That's not good for anyone. There is more to life and it's time for you to start living beyond the garage and these four walls. Pauletta is a beautiful woman and since her recent divorce, she's looking to take a swim in the dating pool as well. What do you say?"

"Have you seen this woman, Scottie?"

"Nah man, but I know that my girl here doesn't associate with dogs."

Vince rubbed his head as if the idea of a date was painful. "Fine, when do y'all want to go on this so called double date?"

"Tomorrow," Haley beamed. "I just called Pauletta to see if she would be free and she said yes. I figured the four of us could go to Lyric Lounge, have a drink or two and listen to some poets do a little spoken word. Doesn't that sound nice?"

"I guess," Vince replied with hesitation.

"Great. Then it's a date." Haley then turned to Scottie, "Babe, I've got some therapy notes to go over tonight so I'm going to head on home."

"If I promise to be quiet while you work can I go with you?" Scottie asked with a devilish grin on his face.

"Okay, but you better be a good boy," Haley whispered as she teased him with a kiss.

"Oh for the love of God, would y'all take all that elsewhere before I get sick?" Vince pretended to be nauseous as the love birds hurried out of the house. He cleaned up his mess and muttered to himself, "What have I gotten myself into?" The next evening as Vince laid his clothes out for his date, he couldn't help but wonder if he was really ready to take this kind of leap. The clothes he'd chosen to wear had been purchased for him by Rozalla. He stepped out of the shower and wiped the steam from the mirror. He looked at his reflection and reasoned with himself that what he was doing was okay. "You didn't put any of this into motion, Rozalla did," he whispered.

The Lyric Lounge was packed as usual. It was the premier spot for Atlanta's best known poets. Vince walked through the crowded venue on the heels of Scottie and Haley. Feeling like a goofy third wheel, he was anxious to get to their small table. Little did he know that he'd caught the eye of several single women who viewed him as anything but goofy. Over the years, he'd maintained his tall, lean physique. The slight hint of gray that accented his short haircut right at the temples made him look sexy and distinguished. Clearly he hadn't given himself enough credit when it came to his appearance. He sported a blue a white button down that hung casually on the outside of his dark jeans. The blue sport coat and dark brown Cole Haan loafers were the cherry that topped off his perfect ensemble.

Finally taking a seat at their table, Haley leaned over and whispered, "You'd better watch out, these women in here look like they're ready to eat you alive."

"Ok, you can stop trying to make me feel good," Vince blushed.

After the waitress came and took their drink orders, they turned their full attention to the stage and listened attentively as the first poet shared his heart through spoken word. As soon as he finished, the crowd burst into applause and a gorgeous woman approached their table. Vince initially thought it was the waitress returning, until he looked up and his eyes met Pauletta's. Aside from Rozalla, she was the most beautiful woman he'd ever seen. Like Rozalla, she had long, flowing locks and a great body. But unlike his wife, Pauletta was the complexion of a chocolate Hershey's Kiss with amazing hazel eyes. She was a stunner.

Haley jumped to her feet to greet her friend. By the time they released their embrace, the men had stood to greet her as well.

"Pauletta, this is my sweetie, Scottie and this is our friend, Vincent." Haley watched as Vince and Pauletta shook hands. Their gaze lingered as did their handshake. "Okay, how about we take our seats, Haley offered.

They all sat and waited as the waitress carefully placed their drinks on the table and took Pauletta's order. Once she'd walked away, the small talk began. They'd pause each time a new poet took the stage, but the conversation would flow again once the musical intermissions would start. The connection between Vince and Pauletta was immediate and to Haley's dismay, a little too real.

"This is not my idea of crazy. She's acting like she really likes him," Haley whispered to Scottie.

He advised her to let Vince enjoy this time because her friend would surely flip the crazy switch before the night was over. As the night began to wind down, Haley excused herself to the restroom and asked that Pauletta join her. Once inside the ladies room, Haley turned to her friend to provide some clarification as to what she was supposed to be doing.

"Okay Pauletta, you've been charming enough. We're closing the night out and you haven't turned on any of the crazy. Remember, you're supposed to be a little coo-coo. We're trying to drive this man back to his wife. Please don't lose sight of the mission."

"Well you should've warned me about how gorgeous and sweet he is. I didn't expect this connection that we clearly have. I thought I was meeting some potbellied, balding guy with the personality of a sponge. You didn't tell me he was so handsome or that he was a successful mechanic. He's a catch!"

"He is married and vulnerable and you're a therapist. We had a plan and I need for you to hold up your end of it. Where is your professionalism?" Haley asked in a raised voice.

"I am a professional, but he is not my patient, nor is he yours. That makes him fair game. I understand your desire to drive him back to his wife, but shame on her dumb ass for letting him go. Her loss is about to be my gain."

CHAPTER THIRTY-TWO

Amanda was seated at her desk rifling through paperwork when her coworker, Nathan Bishop knocked on the door and stepped into her office. They had a good working relationship that had recently blossomed into a great friendship. They laughed together, shared their past hurts, and hopes for the future with one another. And ever since Amanda told Nathan of her best friend's dream where they had become a couple, he'd been trying to convince her that dreams can come true. She knew that he was serious, but continued to blow off his hints and chatter about moving their relationship to a new level.

"What are you doing for dinner tonight, Beautiful?"

Amanda smiled as she always did at the sound of his baritone voice. "Probably just going to heat up some leftovers from last night."

"You mean that stale homemade pizza crap?" Nathan asked with a twisted face.

"Excuse you! My homemade pizza is delicious."

"Yeah, whatever," he uttered with a smirk. "Why don't you join me instead? I've got a serious taste for some jerk chicken with rice and peas."

"Ooh, that does sound good and far be it for me to turn down a free meal," Amanda smiled.

Nathan couldn't help but laugh, "You are so greedy to be so slim, but I love that appetite. Nothing like a woman that enjoys food as much as I do. I'll meet you in the garage at six."

"Okay, Nathan, see you then." Amanda dropped her head and resumed her work as he made his exit from her office. She sifted through her papers, but as hard as she tried she couldn't concentrate on anything related to work- except Nathan. He'd walked out of her office, but stayed on her mind. Checking the clock, Amanda noted that she only had two hours before she'd get to enjoy a nice meal and conversation with the man taking up space in her head and slowly moving into her heart.

Across town, Vince had just made plans of his own with Pauletta. This would be their third date since their initial meeting. He was completely infatuated with her and had convinced himself that his ability to fall for her so easily was a sure sign that his decision to divorce Rozalla was the right one. Unfortunately, he hadn't really been able to convince anyone else. Though he was enjoying Pauletta's company, he would still find ways and reasons to mention his wife's name. He'd only seen her a few times, but spoke of her as if he saw her every day. When Scottie or Haley would point it out to him, he'd just wave them away and say that they were looking for something that no longer existed. They were looking for signs of love between him and Rozalla, but that all the love had evaporated. Needless to say that he was trying to convince himself of that more than he was anyone else.

The small Caribbean restaurant was packed as usual. It hadn't taken long for word to get out about their tasty offerings and now it was almost impossible to get in without a lengthy wait. Luckily, Nathan knew one of the owners and a small corner table was waiting for him and Amanda as soon as they walked through the door. They perused the menu even though they both already knew what they wanted. Nathan got the meal he'd been longing for all day while Amanda opted for the oxtails and rice. After the waitress took their order, they listened to the soft music that wafted through the air and mixed with the aroma of the delicious food that was being served to the satisfied patrons. The couple shared silly glances with each other before picking up conversation about work and everything else that may have crossed their minds.

"You are so silly," Amanda blurted out as she tossed her head back in laughter. But when she raised back up, her laughter stopped cold and her entire expression changed.

"Who the hell is that?" She asked with venom dripping from her words.

"Who is who? What's wrong?" Nathan quizzed as his eyes followed the direction of Amanda intense stare.

"That's my friend, Rozalla's husband, but what I want to know is who that chick is that he's drooling over?"

"Okay, you're looking at her like you want to cut her. Maybe they're just friends trying to get a meal. You know, kind of like us," Nathan offered.

Amanda took note of how Vince was holding the woman's hand, the way she was whispering in his ear and the silly grin plastered across both their faces.

"Are you seriously going to try and tell me that they are just a couple of old friends hanging out after work? If so, I've got a prime piece of property in the everglades I'd like to sell you."

"Alright, so clearly they are more than friends, but in all fairness, he's made his intentions to divorce Rozalla quite clear."

"It's a big difference between saying you're getting a divorce and actually doing it. No papers have been filed and that little fact makes this date of his wrong. I can't believe he's having an affair! This is so out of character for Vince because I know he still loves Roz."

"He may love her, Amanda, but from all you've told me she hurt him bad. She emasculated the man in every way possible. I mean damn, she told him to drop dead."

"But she never cheated, never even considered stepping outside of their marriage. And it's a big difference between having a hateful mouth and committing adultery," Amanda ranted. She took a couple of deep breaths and decided that she had to say something to Vince, she had to let him know that his little secret was out.

"I'll be right back."

Nathan grabbed her hand as she stood to her feet and tried to reason with her. "Amanda, not here. Call him tomorrow or something, but don't make a scene."

"I'm not going to make a scene," she assured him. "But I am going to say something." She gently pulled her hand away and trotted off in Vince's direction.

Pauletta saw Amanda approaching before Vince did and immediately threw up her defenses. She could tell by the way Amanda was strutting in their direction and the scowl on her face that her purpose wasn't to deliver a friendly hello.

"Vince. Fancy seeing you here. How are you?" Amanda asked as she stepped right in front of the pair.

Vince immediately released Pauletta's hand as if he were trying to create some separation between them. "Amanda, what a surprise seeing you here. How are you?" He pulled her into a brief embrace.

Stone faced, Amanda replied, "I'm fine, how are you and who is this?"

Vince stumbled and stuttered over his words, but finally managed to say, "Oh, this is just Pauletta. She's a friend."

Amanda gave her the once over and took note of the tightness in Pauletta's jaw, the anger that had masked her face.

"Humph, nice to meet you, Pauletta," she smirked as she turned her attention back to Vince. "It was good to see you, Vince. I'll be sure and let your wife and kids know that I bumped into you." Amanda turned on her heels and sauntered back off to her table. Just as she took her seat, Vince and his so called friend were darting out the door.

"Damn girl. What did you say to that man to run him off like that?" Nathan asked with a furrowed brow.

"All I did was say hello and that I'd be sure and let Rozalla know that I'd seen him. But from the look on his date's face, I'm the least of his worries."

CHAPTER THIRTY-THREE

Vince dashed out of the restaurant behind a furious Pauletta. His mind was racing trying to understand why she'd suddenly become so angry. It's not like he'd failed to introduce her or forgot her name for goodness sake. Still confused, he opened the car door for her and waited until she was situated to close it back. He then ran around to the driver's side and attempted to get in, but she'd locked the doors. Vince looked at her as if to ask *'What the hell?'* He unlocked the doors with the key fob, but she locked them right back with the inside button.

"Pauletta, this is childish! Stop locking the doors," Vince yelled. He hit the fob again and managed to open the door before she could lock it again. "Are you serious? I mean how old are you because that was the behavior of a five year old!" Vince's voice dripped with annoyance.

Pauletta twisted her body to face him as he slid into the driver's seat. "Maybe it was childish, but what do you expect when you're stumbling all over yourself as if you'd been caught doing something wrong. And when did you decide that we're just friends? I have enough friends and thought that we were dating with a purpose."

Vince looked at her with furrowed brow, put the car in drive, and turned his attention to the road as he cautiously pulled away from the curb. He was too scared to ask what purpose she was referring to. Didn't she realize that all of this was very new to him? He was simply dipping a toe in the dating pool to test the waters and that was his only purpose.

"Are you seriously going to ignore my question? Are you looking to be with me for friendship only?"

"Honestly, Pauletta I haven't really thought about what we'd be. I thought that we were simply getting to know one another and enjoying each other's company." Vince took a deep breath and braced himself for her reply. "What did you think the purpose of our situation was?"

"So now we've gone from friends to a situation?"

The annoyance in Vince's voice was as clear as a bell. "Pauletta, can we not split hairs? You can call it friends, a situation or whatever you like, but would you please just answer the question without all the extra?"

"In all honesty, I thought we were building a relationship. I thought we were both looking for someone to love, looking to build a lasting partnership cemented in love and trust."

Vince drove down the dark street wondering where she'd gotten all these crazy ideas. "You realize that I'm still married. Wouldn't you want my divorce to be settled for at least a year before getting serious with me? I know that's what I would want if the tables were turned. I would never want to be anyone's rebound."

Pauletta had no response and an awkward silence fell between them and lasted for the remainder of the drive to her house. Vince turned into her driveway and killed the ignition. Always the gentleman, he jumped out of the car, dashed to the passenger side to open the door for her and escort her to the house.

"I'm sorry about the way the night turned out. I only wanted to share a good meal and conversation. I had no way of knowing things would happen the way that they did."

"I know, Vince, but I'm willing to let you make it up to me. Come in for a moment and have a drink with me before you head home."

Not wanting to hurt her feelings any more than he already had, Vince took her key from her hand, opened the door, and escorted her in. Pauletta's house was small, but beautifully appointed. The décor matched her personality perfectly. Everything from the custom curtains to the polished hardwoods and every piece of furniture in between screamed successful, sexy, single female. Now if he could get her to cool her heels on the relationship chatter, she'd be the perfect woman to hang out with.

Pauletta took his hand in hers. "Come on in the kitchen and I'll pour us some wine."

Vince followed her lead and thought how nice it was that they were able to put the earlier blunders of the evening behind so quickly. Maybe, just maybe she wasn't as high strung and desperate as he was thinking she was. He leaned against the granite countertop and watched as she elegantly removed the wine glasses from the cabinet and filled them with merlot. She passed him a glass and then lifted hers for a toast and Vince followed suit.

"Here's to taking things as slow as you'd like and developing an amazing friendship."

Vince was pleasantly surprised by her words and with a smile on his face he replied, "I'll gladly toast to that, Beautiful."

Pauletta took another sip of her wine as she moved closer to Vince. She placed her glass on the counter behind him and cupped his face in her hands. She kissed him seductively, allowing her tongue to dance in and around his mouth. As human nature would have it, he responded in kind. Then suddenly he placed his hands on her wrists and gently pushed her away.

"I'm sorry, Pauletta, but as you know I'm still married. It wouldn't be fair to either of us to continue with this."

Pauletta didn't say a word, in fact she acted as if she hadn't heard a word he'd said. She reached for his waist and started unbuckling his pants. Shocked, Vince pushed her hands away, but she was persistent. He was completely stunned when she managed to get his pants undone and dropped to her knees. Vince's body betrayed him as she proceeded to stroke his manhood. Still, he tried to pull her up from the floor and get her to release his stiffness. But again, she refused and began to pleasure him with her wet mouth. Vince gave up the fight and allowed himself to enjoy the spontaneous blow job. His leg trembled as he released all that had built up over the course of the past couple of months. Pauletta slowly stood up and wiped her mouth as Vince tried to collect himself.

"I know you want to take things slowly, but this is how life could be everyday if we were to take our relationship to the next level. Don't you want to be loved like this, every day, Vince?"

Vince tucked his shirt in and secured his pants with his belt. He'd never experienced a woman being so aggressive. And while he liked what she did, all he could think about was how Rozalla did it so much better.

"Don't you want this, every day, Vince?" Pauletta asked again, snatching him from the memories of his wife.

…ıd want that, Pauletta, but for us it doesn't …ning. I'm sorry, but I'm not an adulterer and until …lage is legally dissolved, nothing like this can happen …ı. Do you understand?"

"Get out," Pauletta said softly.

"I'm sorry, what did you say?"

"I said get the hell out of my house!" she screamed at the top of her lungs. "I'm not your whore and you won't keep using me. Now get the hell out! Get out," she continued to scream as she pushed Vince towards the front door. "You're just like every other man, a selfish user. Get out!" She literally pushed Vince onto the porch and slammed the door.

Vince was in a complete state of shock. He looked around to see if anyone else was around. Was there a hidden camera, was he being pranked? Surely this had to be a joke because no one was really this crazy. But as he looked around and saw no one, he walked to his car and headed in the direction of Scottie's place. He replayed the evening over and over again in his head as he drove down the highway. He may not have known what motivated Pauletta to behave the way she had, but he was pretty sure that he'd never hear from her again and that was just fine with him.

CHAPTER THIRTY-FOUR

"Hey girl!" Rozalla squealed as she slid into the passenger seat of Amanda's car. "I'm so glad you called. I feel like I've been cooped up in the house forever. A girls night out is just what I need."

Amanda checked her rearview mirror as she backed out of the driveway. A nervous smile was plastered on her face because she knew that this wouldn't be the exciting girl's night out that her friend was anticipating. "Roz, you know we're just going to grab a bite to eat, it's not like we're hitting the club," Amanda chuckled.

"I don't care if we go to McDonalds and eat in their play area. I'm just excited to be out of the house and sharing a meal with someone. Trust me when I say that talking to the television is overrated."

"Well I think we can do a little better that McDonald's and unlike your television, I talk back."

Rozalla chuckled at her friend's comment and began to chat about insignificant things. Amanda merged onto the highway and headed for The Capital Grill, but hadn't responded to anything else Rozalla had said. She looked as if she were a million miles away. Rozalla wondered what could possibly be wrong. It wasn't like Amanda to be so quiet or uptight.

"What's the matter, Amanda? You're as quiet as a church mouse and as nervous as a long tail cat in a room full of rocking chairs."

"Oh goodness, you and your little country sayings."

"Yeah, I'm a real hoot. Now tell me what's wrong."

Amanda took a long, deep breath before she spoke the words that she knew would break her friend's heart. "I was having dinner with Nathan last night at a small eatery when Vince came waltzing through the door." Amanda paused, "He wasn't alone."

"Who was he with?" Rozalla asked as nonchalantly as she could, but the crack in her voice made it clear that she was bothered by the news.

"He was with some woman named Pauletta. He seemed real nervous when I went and spoke to him. He said that she was just a friend. That comment didn't seem to sit too well with her and they immediately left the restaurant."

"So what did she look like? How old do you think she was?" There were so many questions swirling around in Rozalla's head, but those were the only two she could manage to get out of her mouth.

"What difference does it make?"

"Amanda, please…"

"I don't see the point of this, but I would guess she's in her late thirties, average height, dark completed, kind of cute I suppose."

"I bet she had long hair," Rozalla grunted.

"You would win that bet." As they approached the restaurant Amanda tried to anticipate Rozalla's next question. She hoped there would be no more questions about the woman's looks. Amanda had played down her stunning features as best she could.

No more questions were hurled at her because her best friend was too busy wiping the tears from her eyes.

"Roz, this isn't worth crying over. For all we know they really are just friends."

"Nah, Vince has maintained a lifelong philosophy that men and women can't be just friends. I don't see why he'd change his way of thinking now." Rozalla dabbed her eyes with a tissue and shook her head in disbelief.

"I know he said he wanted a divorce, but I never would've thought that he'd start dating before the divorce was final. He's always believed so strongly in the sanctity of marriage and honoring our wedding vows."

"I don't think he's thinking very clearly, Roz. And again, the woman got upset when he acknowledged her as a friend. Maybe she wants more but he doesn't." Amanda believed what she was saying, but more importantly, she wanted Roz to believe it.

It wasn't long before they reached their destination. Amanda killed the engine to the car and turned to face Rozalla who was still dabbing tears from her eyes.

"If you're not up for this, Roz we can grab some take out and head back to my house. We can have an old fashioned slumber party," Amanda offered. It was her feeble attempt to lighten the mood.

Rozalla chuckled, "No offense, but you're not who I want to spend the night with." She pulled down the visor, grabbed the pressed powder from her purse, and touched up her makeup. "I'm hungry and I'd like a drink. Let's go in."

It didn't take long for the ladies to be seated. They each enjoyed a cocktail before their meals arrived to the table. Rozalla managed to put Vince and his date out of her mind long enough to hear the details of Amanda's advancing relationship with Nathan. They were still taking things slow which Rozalla thought was great. It was the sure way to build a strong foundation for a lasting relationship. After a while the conversation took a turn towards work and Rozalla's excitement over returning to the hospital soon. The conversation flowed like water and neither of them ever realized that they were being watched from across the room.

"So have you spoken with Heather? Does she know that you'll be returning to the work soon?"

"Amanda, if she's called me once she's called me a thousand times. I'm sure she knows I'm returning soon, but I've had no interest in talking to her lately. I've had so much time to myself I've been replaying our friendship. Any woman who would bad mouth my marriage and work so hard to convince me that my husband wasn't good enough is not a real friend. I don't need her poisonous attitude and outlook on marriage permeating my life anymore."

"I'm so glad to hear you say that," Amanda confessed as she blew a sigh of relief. Before she could get her next sentence out a woman approached their table. Amanda looked up and was shocked to see their visitor. "Pauletta?"

"Yes, your name is Amanda, right?"

"You know it is. What do you want?"

Rozalla looked back and forth between the women trying to figure out who this beautiful stranger was and why her friend was being so rude.

Pauletta turned her attention to Rozalla, looking at her as if she smelled like two-day old garbage. "Then this must be Vince's beloved wife," she said with a nasty smirk.

"As a matter of fact it is," Amanda confirmed. "And something tells me that when it's all said and done she'll remain his beloved wife."

"I wouldn't bet on it."

"Heifer, I don't know who the hell you think you are, but I will mop the floor with you," Rozalla said as she stood to face Pauletta straight on. "I will tell you this one time only, leave me and my husband alone."

"And I will tell you this one time only, Vince is going to be mine. You just get your pen ready to sign those divorce papers, bitch."

Rozalla lunged at Pauletta, but Amanda grabbed her by the arm and pulled her to her seat.

Pauletta looked over her shoulder laughing. "That's right, control that animal." She continued laughing wickedly as she walked out of the doors of the restaurant.

"Let me guess, that was Vince's friend from last night," Rozalla said as she gathered herself.

"Good guess, my friend. Good guess." Amanda rubbed her temples and tried to mentally prepare for all the hell that was about to break loose.

CHAPTER THIRTY-FIVE

Vince had successfully dodged Scottie and Haley for the last couple of days. He had no idea what Pauletta had shared with Haley, but he was about to find out. They were both home and he knew he couldn't avoid a conversation with them any longer. He took a deep breath and exited his truck. When he'd agreed to the blind date, he thought it might result in a friend he could occasionally have dinner with at most. But now he had to tell Haley that her friend wanted far more from him than he was willing to give.

"Well look who the cat drug in," Scottie teased. "Man, we've been missing each other left and right. What's been going on with you?"

"Babe, let the man get in the door and relax a minute before you start hitting him with questions," Haley interjected.

Vince dropped his keys on the end table and plopped into the chair that sat opposite of the happy couple. He could see the anticipation all over their faces and a glint of excitement in Haley's eyes. Had she not talked to Pauletta? Had Pauletta lied and told her that they had a fabulous date and ended the night with a round of passionate sex? He hated to burst Haley's bubble, but he had no choice.

"You two look like you're anticipating Santa Claus," Vince chuckled, trying to lighten his own mood.

"That's what it feels like to me," Haley confessed. "Now give me my gift. Tell me that I'm the matchmaking champion."

"If I were looking for a serious, long term relationship, I'd say that you're the champ. However, y'all know that I'm not ready to get involved in anything heavy. I was hoping for a friend to share an occasional meal and conversation with. Pauletta is clearly looking for more. I'm sorry, Haley, but your friend is too much for me."

Scottie looked at Vince suspiciously, he knew from the look on his buddy's face that there was more to the story. "What makes you think she wants something more than friendship?" he asked.

Vince rubbed his hands together nervously. "Maybe this is conversation we should have when we're not in the presence of a lady."

"Vince please, I've seen and heard it all. I need to know what happened, I need to know what Pauletta did to turn you off so quickly. I mean everything seemed fine initially. What changed?" Haley had a mix of confusion and annoyance etched across her face.

A deep breath escaped through Vince's lips as he maneuvered his body to the edge of his seat. "Everything was going well until a couple of nights ago. We went out to eat and Amanda happened to be there. When she came over to speak, I introduced Pauletta as a friend. To say she got pissed would be a major understatement. She immediately walked out of the restaurant. The closer we got to her place, the calmer she seemed to get and even invited me in. Once inside she very forcibly performed fellatio on me. I tried to get her stop, tried to pull her up off of her knees, but she was determined. When she was done and started talking about a serious relationship again, I told her that I was still married and didn't believe in adultery. She went off, threw me out and everything. I won't lie and say that I wasn't relieved. She's a different kind of crazy and I can't, I won't deal with it."

"Man, did she give good head?"

"Seriously, Scottie," Haley scolded. "I'm sorry, Vince, I had no idea. When she came to work yesterday she was all smiles. She didn't go into detail about your date, but she gave the impression that you two had an amazing time."

"No need for apologies, Haley. I appreciate what you were trying to do, but clearly I'm not ready to date. I've got to resolve things with my wife first."

Scottie looked at Haley and smirked, "Well, your plan kind of worked."

"What plan?" Vince asked suspiciously.

Haley starting wringing her hands like a nervous child anticipating punishment from a parent. "I had the bright idea to set you up with Pauletta as a way of getting you to realize that you still loved Rozalla and needed to work things out with her. Pauletta knew that this was the plan and she was all for it, but once she saw you, she decided that you were a good catch for real. I'm sorry, Vince, this little trick had worked before and I thought it would again. I had no idea that she would get all crazy on you. But rest assured, I'll make sure that she leaves you alone."

"It's okay, Haley, I know your heart was in the right place. Hopefully she'll go away without any intervention. But like you said, Scottie, it kind of worked because I realize now that I can't keep putting things off with Rozalla. I've got to talk to her…" Before he could finish his thought, his cell phone rang. "Speak of the devil, it's Rozalla. Excuse me." Vince stood and walked towards his bedroom as he answered the phone. "Hello."

"Hi Vince. How are you?"

"I'm fine, Roz. How are you?"

"I'm actually a little upset and I really need to talk to you. Would you please come by the house?"

"Sure. Give me about an hour." Vince disconnected the call and looked at his reflection in the mirror.

"Here we go," he said, figuring that Amanda had told his wife about his little date.

About thirty minutes later Vince emerged from his room, freshly showered and dressed casually. When he stepped into the kitchen, Haley couldn't help but admire how handsome and fit he was. Though she didn't agree with Pauletta's behavior, looking at Vince she certainly understood her attraction.

"Wish me luck. Rozalla called and said she was a little upset and asked if I could come over. We all know that Amanda told her about seeing me out with Pauletta. Hopefully I won't get cursed out too badly," Vince chuckled.

Scottie walked around the counter and gave Vince a brother man hug. "Stay strong man and if she pulls a knife, run like the wind."

"Oh my goodness, Scottie, cut all that foolishness out. Vince, talk to your wife. Be honest with her. Most importantly, be honest with yourself about whether you really want to dissolve your marriage."

"I hear you, Haley. I'll see you guys later." Vince turned and walked out of the house. He jumped in his truck, turned the radio to the Jazz station and headed towards his home. He never noticed the Toyota driven by a woman in dark sunglasses and a black baseball cap following him. When he pulled into he and Rozalla's driveway, the Toyota parked against the curb diagonally across the street. The woman slumped down in her seat as Vince strolled to the front door and let himself in.

As soon as he crossed the threshold he knew that Rozalla was in the kitchen. The aroma of food drew him to her like it always did. She cooked like no other and she knew that good food was his weakness.

"Hey Roz," he timidly greeted her with a light kiss on the cheek. "It smells great in here!"

"Hi Vince. I thought that we could have a little talk over dinner. I figured a good meal would make our chat a little less painful," she half-heartedly teased. "I hope you're in the mood for parmesan crusted chicken, baked potato, and sautéed spinach."

"That's sounds great, but I could've sworn I smelled something sweet too."

Rozalla couldn't help but laugh. "Still have that sweet tooth, huh?"

"You know some things will never change."

"Well depending on how this conversation goes, there may be peach cobbler and ice cream for dessert. Now do me a favor and fill a couple of glasses with ice while I fix our plates."

After praying over their meal, Vince picked up his fork and asked Rozalla to speak her mind as he dug into his food.

"I don't need to tell you that Amanda told me about your date. You already knew that she would. But what you don't know is that I got to meet Miss Pauletta for myself."

Vince almost choked on his food. He turned beet red as he coughed and tried to regain his composure. "What do you mean you met Pauletta?"

Rozalla recounted the events of the previous day. She could see anger rise up within Vince as she told him about Pauletta calling her a bitch and declaring that Vince would be hers. Before he spoke a word, Rozalla knew that this Pauletta chick held no space in Vince's heart.

"Roz, I am so sorry. I never imagined that anything like this would happen. That woman is an associate of Haley's. Haley and Scottie had the idea that if they hooked me up with her, I'd realize how much I love and miss you. The whole plan went awry and now we all see that she's a little nuts. I've told her that I have no interest in a relationship and that revelation got me kicked out of her house. I guess that's why I'm so shocked to hear that she actually approached you like that."

Rozalla continued to eat her meal as she absorbed his words. She was relieved that he didn't want Pauletta, but that didn't mean that he wanted her either. Did he still want a divorce? She swallowed her fear with a fork full of spinach and asked, "So where does all this leave us? Do you still a divorce?"

Vince reached for his wife's hand. He caressed it and gently twirled the wedding band that still made her hand it's home. "Roz, you know that I still love you. It's impossible to forget all the happy years that we've shared, but the last couple of years was more than I could take. I never stopped treating you well or trying to make you happy, but you turned on me, Baby. You talked to and about me like I was dog, like you'd forgotten that I loved you. You can't imagine how bad it hurt when you told me you wished I were dead. That remark cut like a knife."

Rozalla was using her napkin to catch the tears that were racing from her eyes. She knew that everything he was saying was true and she had no one to blame but herself. She allowed herself to be influenced by her so called friend, Heather. But the blame and shame still fell flatly at her feet because no grown ass woman should allow herself to be negatively influenced by anyone. She should know and follow her own mind.

"I am beyond sorry for my behavior. The last couple of years have been the greatest regret of my life. I'll never be able to apologize enough, Vince. I was stupid, selfish, and I am completely ashamed of my behavior. I should've listened to you when you said that you didn't trust Heather. I'm so sorry."

"Look, I don't want you feel like you've got to keep apologizing. What I need to know is that whatever or whomever made you turn on me is no longer a part of your life. I need to know that you are mentally stable and not going to pull anymore fake suicide attempts. All of that behavior was so far from the Roz I know and love and I refuse to deal with it."

Rozalla squeezed his hand and assured him that all of that was behind her. She even suggested that they reconnect slowly, start dating again and give themselves a chance to remember why they fell in love in the first place. The broad smile plastered across Vince's face let her know that he loved the idea. He leaned across the table and kissed her gently, but before he could kiss her again, they heard a loud bang outside the kitchen window. Vince jumped up to see what it was, but there was nothing there except for a turned over trash can. He figured the neighbor's cat must've gotten out again. He returned to the table just as Rozalla was dishing up dessert.

CHAPTER THIRTY-SIX

"Damn it! Damn it, damn it, damn it," Pauletta shouted over and over as she pounded her steering wheel with both hands. She took a deep breath and started the car as she continued to rant her anger.

"I can't believe he's over here sharing a meal with this bitch, kissing her and holding her hand." She sped off down the street. Completely consumed with rage, she almost hit an oncoming car head on. The car swerved and landed in a ditch, but that didn't stop Pauletta from screaming a string of obscenities out of her window at them.

The thirty-minute drive to the office did nothing to curb Pauletta's anger. With it being Sunday, she assumed she'd have the building to herself. She wanted to rifle through Haley's things to see if she could find the address where Vince was staying or any other information she might have on him, but to her surprise, Haley was in her office. Pauletta tried to ease back out without being noticed, but her attempt fail miserably.

"Pauletta," Haley called as she signaled for her to come into the office. "What are you doing here on a Sunday afternoon?"

"I could ask you the same thing," Pauletta replied.

The smile on Pauletta's face could not hide the anger in her voice. "What's wrong? You sound really bothered. Is it anything I can help with?" Haley quizzed.

"No, I've just got some things on my mind. I thought I could come here and be alone to think."

"I'm sorry I ruined your alone time, but I thought I'd come in and catch up on some patient reports. You know, you do live alone and your beautiful home is in a quiet neighborhood," Haley offered.

"Thank you, Haley! Thank you for the reminder that I'm all alone and have no one to share my home with. I'm glad you've got your precious Scottie, but damn it, don't rub your relationship in my face!" Pauletta's voice trembled as angry tears ran down her face.

Haley walked around her desk and attempted to wrap Pauletta in her arms and comfort her through whatever she was going through. But to her surprise, Pauletta pushed her away and stared at her with cold, evil eyes.

"This is all your fault," Pauletta spat. "You set me up with this man that you knew was still in love with his wife. You put a plan into motion that would leave me hurt and alone."

"Pauletta, you knew that this was all supposed to be a ploy to get Vince to realize how much he still loved and wanted to be with his wife. What is wrong with you? We've done this before. You were never supposed to have a relationship with Vince. Don't blame me for your feelings when you were never supposed to develop any in the first place. You flipped the script, not me!"

"I don't even know why I'm talking to you about this, Haley. Just forget my feelings and go back to your perfect little life. I'll fend for myself as I always have," Pauletta declared. "But I do have one simple request."

Haley leaned back on her desk with her arms crossed. Her annoyance was quite evident. "What is it, Pauletta?"

"I just want to know where Vince is staying."

"Why?"

"Because I want to talk to him if that okay with you! I deserve that much. Tell me where he's staying so that we can have a conversation and end this thing amicably."

"End what thing, Pauletta? You two never had anything. You went on a couple of dates, that's all."

"It was more than that, we made love."

"No, you gave him head thinking that it would make him stay. It was a pathetic, juvenile move that backfired. Let it go, he doesn't want you and his whereabouts are neither of our business. If you want a conversation, call him and ask for one. But be warned, he will tell you no."

Pauletta became enraged. Without warning she lunged at Haley, grabbing her around the throat with both hands. She literally dragged Haley from one end of her desk to the other, sending all that sat neatly atop it crashing to the floor. Haley tried desperately to free herself from Pauletta's grasp, but it was a passing security guard that wrestled her off and pinned her to the floor. Pauletta struggled to free herself as she screamed a string of obscenities at the security guard.

Haley managed to catch her breath, retrieve the phone, and call 911. In the six minutes it took for the police to arrive, Pauletta never stopped cursing or struggling to free herself from the security guard's grip. Even as the cops handcuffed her and ushered her out of the building, Pauletta vowed to pay Haley back and to make Vince hers. Haley was still shocked and confused by Pauletta's behavior and she couldn't deny the little twinge of fear.

CHAPTER THIRTY-SEVEN

Heather waited patiently for Rozalla's shift to end. It was her intent to catch her old friend as she exited the hospital. She had tried numerous times to get Rozalla to have dinner, lunch or drinks with her, but Roz had shut her down each time. She couldn't understand for the life of her what she'd done that made Roz no longer interested in a friendship with her. The elevator dinged and Heather looked up just as Roz was stepping out of it. As she started to trot in Rozalla's direction, she could see Roz pretend not to see her and hasten her pace. "Roz, I know you see me. Please slow down, I just want five minutes, that's all, five lousy minutes." Heather breathed a sigh of relief as Roz walked over to a bank of chairs and waited.

"Hi , Heather. I'm sorry. I was kind of in a hurry. What can I do for you?"

"You can tell me what I've done to push you away? We were so cool, but now you won't return my phone calls or texts. You avoid me like the plague. Why?"

"I'm sorry, Heather. I shouldn't have avoided you for so long. You didn't do anything. I've been taking time for myself, reevaluating my relationships and I don't feel that continuing our friendship is in my best interest."

"Why?" Heather asked with confusion etched across her face.

Roz took a deep breath as she mentally reviewed all the things Heather said about Vince, about their marriage. "Heather, I allowed you to speak ill about my husband. Like some little teenager I allowed your words and views on marriage to influence what I felt about Vince. I ignored all he'd been to me and done for me and placed unreasonable expectations on him. I'm not saying it's your fault, but this has made me realize that I need friends that are going to support my marriage. I need to surround myself with friends that are going to offer encouragement and that have a positive outlook on relationships. You don't exactly fall into that category."

"So because I opened your eyes to what was lacking in your marriage, you're going to push me out of your life?"

"Pretty much. If I didn't see any problems with my marriage, it wasn't up to you to create any. I'm sorry Heather, but I have to go. I have a date with my husband." Rozalla turned and headed out of the building while Heather stood there stewing in the anger of the broken friendship.

~~~

Dress after dress flew across the bed. Each one that Rozalla pulled out of the closet seemed inadequate for her date with Vince. She wondered how the other ladies would dress. She already knew that Amanda had exquisite taste in everything and would be dressed in some beautiful ensemble. She didn't, however know anything about Haley. She didn't want to be overdressed, but definitely wanted everyone to take notice of her, especially Vince. She pulled out another dress but dropped it when she heard the front door slam. Rozalla moved across the room and retrieved her baseball bat. She was poised and ready to swing when Lisa and Carmen came barreling through the bedroom door.

Lisa jumped back, almost knocking Carmen over. "What the hell, Mama?" Lisa shouted as she dodged the swing of the bat.

"Oh my goodness," Rozalla screamed as she dropped the bat. "What are y'all doing here? I thought you were a burglar!"

"Dang Mama, we stopped by to see if you wanted to go to dinner with us. And since when did you start keeping a Louisville Slugger by your bed?" Carmen asked.

"Since my family deserted me and left me alone in this big old house."

"No one deserted you, old woman. Now do you want to go to dinner with us or what?"

"Look around Carmen. It looks like she's got other plans for the night," Lisa interjected. "Where are you going and who are you going with?"

Rozalla face relaxed into a broad smile, "Your father."

"Are you serious?" Lisa quizzed. "When did this happen? I mean have you two decided to get back together? Is he moving back in?"

"Cool your heels little girl. He's not moving back in yet, but that is the ultimate goal. We're dating and taking things slow and rebuilding the love and trust that I so stupidly broke down."

"This is awesome, Mama, but I had no idea that you guys were even talking again. How did all of this come about?" Carmen plopped onto her mom's bed anxiously awaiting all of the details.

Rozalla continued to riffle through her closet as she recounted the details of the recent encounters with Pauletta. The girls were shocked to hear that their father had been dating another woman. They were equally as terrified to hear that the woman had turned out to be a psycho.

"I can't believe that witch had the nerve to step to you and Amanda's table, let alone speak to you like that. Clearly she doesn't know who she's dealing with because we will mop the floor with her ass," Lisa ranted.

"What I don't understand is why Scottie and Haley weren't more selective in their choice of women? Did they pull this idiot off of a street corner or what?" Carmen questioned.

"From what I understand she is a mental health professional and works with Haley at a prominent psychiatric clinic. Apparently, the plan was to set him up with another woman to get him to realize how much he still loved me. And before you ask, yes, Pauletta was in on the plan, but when she saw your dad, she changed the plans. How does this dress look?"

Lisa crooked her head and squinted her eyes, "Where are you going?"

"Well, we're meeting Amanda, Nathan, Scottie, and Haley at Sweet Georgia's Juke Joint for dinner and dancing. You know that Amanda will look amazing and I'm sure Haley will too. I want to fit right in, but still stand out a little, if that makes any sense."

"I'll be right back," Carmen said as she jumped up and shot out the door.

Perplexed, Rozalla asked, "What's with her?"

"How should I know? She didn't whisper anything extra to me on the way out."

"You and that smart mouth. All you had to say was I don't know."

"I wouldn't be me if I didn't have this smart mouth," Lisa retorted.

Before Rozalla could form a response, Carmen came busting back into the room carrying a Macy's bag. "Don't ever say that I don't love you, old lady. I just bought this, but it would look so good on you." Carmen pulled a beautiful, sleeveless, purple jumpsuit from the bag. "Mama, you should wear this with that new wide, black belt and black stilettos you got from Dillard's."

"This is so cute, but you don't think it's too casual?" Rozalla asked.

"For goodness sake, you're going to dinner and dancing, not a White House correspondent's dinner. I mean these are nice, but a little too dressy," Lisa interjected. "This jumpsuit is sexy and classy. Daddy's jaw will drop!"

"You sure you don't mind me wearing it, Carmen?"

"If I minded, Mama I never would've brought it in here. Consider it my contribution to you and Daddy mending your marriage."

Lisa and Carmen spend the next thirty minutes helping their mom prepare for her date. When Rozalla slipped into the jumpsuit, the girls were in awe of how gorgeous she looked. Her Hispanic and African American heritage created the most amazing, flawless complexion and her forty-three-year-old body could easily pass for that of a fit thirty-year-old. Rozalla's daughters only hoped that they would age as gracefully. There was a light tap on the front door as Vince eased it open and just as they'd imagined, he was completely taken by his wife's beauty. As they headed out of the door hand-in-hand, they were teased and told to be careful and not bring any new babies into the world.

CHAPTER THIRTY-EIGHT

Sweet Georgia's Juke Joint was packed. Thank God they'd made a reservation. Vince and Rozalla were ushered through the crowd to a table where Scottie and Haley were already seated. Pleasantries were exchanged and drinks were ordered as they waited for Amanda and Nathan to arrive.

Haley cleared her throat and found the courage to apologize to Rozalla. "Roz, I know we're here to have fun, but I need to apologize to you first. When I set Vince up with Pauletta it was supposed to go quite differently. I never imagined that she'd get all crazy and obsessed. It was never my intention to pull you two apart, my stupid plot was intended to do the complete opposite."

Rozalla reached across the table and gave Haley's hand a warm squeeze. "I know that and no apologies are necessary. I mean look at us, despite a little insanity your plan actually worked and for that I'm grateful."

"Are you two going to start singing Kumbaya now?" Amanda joked as she and Nathan approached the table. Everyone laughed and they all exchanged hugs and hellos. Just as Rozalla had said, Amanda was gorgeous. Haley looked beautiful as well, but Roz was confident, happy and outshined them both. The couples made small talk, laughed, ordered drinks and the entire time Vince lovingly held his wife's hand. Everyone at the table took notice and whispered a prayer of thanks for the rekindling of their marriage.

It wasn't long after placing their orders that the meals arrived and the band took the stage. They devoured the food, toasted to friendship, and moved to the beat of the music. The band was playing old school and the lead female singer was phenomenal. The waiter had barely removed their plates before Vince swept Roz off to the small dance floor. It was as if they were newlyweds again, behaving like they did before they had kids. The other couples looked on, but Amanda had a couple questions for Haley before they joined Roz and Vince on the dance floor.

"Haley, I hope you don't mind my bringing this up, but I was wondering if Pauletta has said anything to you regarding Vince. Does she seem like she's backing off?"

"No, I don't mind. I know it's something we've all been concerned about. Amanda, I haven't told either of them this but I had a crazy run in with Pauletta this past Sunday." Haley went on to explain exactly what happened.

"She hasn't been back to work since the police carted her off. I don't even know if she's been bailed out yet. Now I haven't shared this with Vince or Roz yet. Things are progressing so well that I wanted to let them get through tonight before hitting them with more craziness."

"But you do know that they have to be told?" Amanda quizzed.

"Of course and my plan was to tell them over Sunday dinner. I'm cooking and you guys are welcome to join us. Roz might even handle all this better if you're present."

"Baby, I don't think we can wait another two days to tell them," Scottie interjected.

"Why?"

"Look who just bellied up to the bar." All heads turned to see Pauletta eyeballing the dance floor.

"Aww damn!" Haley dropped her head in disgust.

"You have got to be kidding! Do you think she followed them here?" Amanda questioned to no one in particular and no one answered. They all had their sights locked on her and she had her sights locked on Vince and Rozalla. Pauletta tossed back a Martini while she glared in envy at the happy couple.

"I just pray that she doesn't cause a scene," Haley added.

Scotties grunted, "There will be none of that shit in here tonight." He glared at Pauletta until she could feel someone's eyes burrowing through her. She turned and saw the table full of her obsession's friends. The way they eyeballed her reminded her of southern lynch mob ready to hang their prey. She glared back at them with disdain, but their message was still very clear. She raised her glass in a toast towards their table, guzzled the alcohol down, gathered her purse, and left. Everyone's eyes followed her out the door.

"What are y'all staring at?" Rozalla asked as she and Vince returned to their seats.

Everyone looked at them, but no one spoke. Finally, Nathan spoke up, "A familiar and unpleasant face surfaced in the crowd and we just wanted to make sure that it disappeared out the door."

Rozalla look completely confused. "Who was it?"

All eyes fell to Haley as she sighed deeply, hating to ruin what was supposed to be a beautiful evening. "It was Pauletta. We don't know if she followed you here or if she just showed up by chance. Either way, it didn't take her long to spot you two on the dance floor and eyes didn't leave you until Scottie managed to get her attention. When she realized we were all here, she got her stuff and left."

As the band took a much deserved break, the waiter approached the table to see if anyone wanted another drink. Vince, seemingly undisturbed by the news of Pauletta, ordered a bottle of wine for the table.

"We're not going to allow anyone or anything to ruin this evening. Yes, that woman is clearly crazy as hell, but this woman," he said as he gently too Rozalla's hand.

"This woman has captivated my heart all over again. I clearly remember why I fell so hard for her in the first place. An evening like this is what we needed and we will enjoy it. So if it's all the same with you guys, we won't discuss the crazy one anymore this evening."

The others had no choice but to honor the law that Vince had laid down. The talk that Haley had planned for Sunday would go on as planned, but the remainder of this evening would hold nothing but joy and happiness. When the band returned, all of the couples hit the floor and danced the night away.

After everyone departed, Rozalla and Vince drove the city streets listening to jazz and holding hands. Despite the small hiccup, they had enjoyed the evening and Vince had no plans for the night to end. Once they reached the house, he walked Rozalla to the door and decided to invite himself in. He knew that they'd agreed to take things slow, but his wife was looking too good for him to be able to keep his hands off of her. As soon as he locked the front door behind them, he pulled Roz into a passionate kiss. His hands roamed through her long, thick curls and slowly, methodically made their way down to her neck and shoulders and his kisses followed. With each kiss and nibble her breath quickened and heartbeat raced. It had been a long time and the anticipation excited her beyond words. Vince escorted her to their bedroom where they kissed, fondled, and undressed one another.

Vince stepped back to take in the fullness of his wife's full breasts, curvaceous hips. She was as beautiful now as she was all those years ago. Rozalla stepped to him, kissed him deeply as she led him to the bed, and laid down with her legs open and inviting. Vince eased himself between her caramel thighs and made love to his wife the way he knew she loved him to. Hitting all the right spots while whispering all the right words. It was so incredible that when they done, he fell asleep in her. They stayed connected for hours.

CHAPTER THIRTY-NINE

Slowly Amanda turned over in bed. She didn't want to open her eyes yet, it was Saturday and she was trying to will herself to fall back asleep and rejoice in not having to go to work. But as the reality of where she was dawned on her, she opened her eyes, sat up and looked around. The bed, the room, the house didn't belong to her. She'd had no intentions of staying over at Nathan's, but that's exactly what had happened. She tried to recount the evening from the time they walked into his house up to now. All the wine she'd consumed had her memory a little more than fuzzy.

It was so unlike her to drink so much. She remembered them laughing and kissing, but she was afraid of what else had happened. It's not like she was still in her clothes, they were draped over a chair in the corner. Instead, one of Nathan's t-shirts covered her body. She dropped her head in her hands and wondered what he must think of her. They'd agreed to take things slow, to allow their feelings to build before allowing lust to take over. But clearly she'd failed and given herself to this man. Surely his respect level for her had plummeted.

"Wait, where is he?" She asked herself as she listened for sounds to creep in from another area of the house. When she heard nothing, she decided that this was a prime opportunity to get dressed and slither out before he returned from wherever he'd crept off to. Clothes on, purse and keys in hand, Amanda hastily moved towards the front door. But just before she reached it, Nathan came waltzing through it.

"Good morning, Gorgeous. Were you trying to sneak out on me?" He asked with a slight chuckle.

Amanda stumbled over her words before finally responding. "I wasn't sure where you were and didn't want to interfere with your plans for the day. Besides, I've got errands to run and need to go home and shower."

"Hmm, well lucky for you I have no plans for the day. I did a quick run to the store so that I could make us a little breakfast. I even purchased some K-Cups of your favorite flavored coffee. Oh, and I got you a toothbrush because I know that morning breathe has to be kicking," he joked as he handed her a new, pink Colgate toothbrush.

"Thank you, Nathan, but I really think it's best if I go," Amanda spoke with her head down, willing to look anywhere but into Nathan's eyes.

"What's wrong, Amanda? Why are you acting all weird?"

"Look, I'm a little embarrassed and feeling really stupid right now. I just need a little time to deal with my feelings and get myself together. I promise to call you later," she said as she attempted to move towards the door.

"No, no, this is not how we're going to start this relationship. We're going to do things right and talk through any issues." He took her by the hand and led her to the kitchen. "Here, take a seat and talk to me while I fix us a bite to eat."

Amanda sat there but didn't say a word. She was embarrassed and didn't know where to start. How could she speak on how beautiful last night was when she didn't even remember it? How could she make him believe that drinking too much and having random sex wasn't her regular mode of operation?

"Babe, you're not saying anything. At least tell me why you were really trying to creep up out of here."

"I'm so embarrassed to have to admit this, but I have no recollection of last night beyond our sitting down with that bottle of wine. I can't recall our conversation, let alone getting undressed and making love to you," she mumbled with her eyes fixated on the floor. She only bothered to look up when she heard Nathan laughing.

"Really, you're going to laugh at my stupidity?"

"First of all, you're not stupid and secondly, if you'd made love to me, I promise you'd remember every second of it. Hell, you'd be tearing at my clothes right now begging for seconds," he chuckled. "Because baby I've got that good loving." He began to move his waist as if he were having sex with the air.

Amanda looked on and couldn't help but smile at his silly antics. "You mean to tell me that I've been beating myself up for having sex with you when nothing really happened?"

"That's what I'm telling you, gorgeous."

"Then how did I get in your t-shirt?"

"Oh, I did help you out of your clothes and into the shirt, but I did it with only one eye open. You know I'm telling the truth 'cause your bra and panties were still on."

"So nothing happened?"

"No ma'am, when we throw down for the first time I'm going to need you wide awake and fully functioning so you can scream my name and scratch my back."

Amanda almost fell out of her chair laughing. "You are so foolish!"

"I'm so serious. Now please go brush your teeth. I cannot enjoy my food while in the presence of funky breath," Nathan joked as he continued to beat the eggs. He watched as Amanda walked towards the bathroom with toothbrush in hand and couldn't help but hope for the day when they actually would make love. She was smart, beautiful, had goals, and would undoubtedly be there for her man. As they spent more time together, he found himself not just wanting more of her, but all of her. Amanda was phenomenal and all he wanted was to make her happy.

She practically danced back into the kitchen. Music was now playing and since learning the truth about last night, Amanda felt as if she'd shed a hundred pounds. She kissed Nathan on the cheek. "Is that better?"

"Much! Do me a favor and grab a couple of cups out of the cabinet up there and pour us some coffee."

"Sure thing. You want cream and sugar?"

"The sweeter the better," he replied with a wink. He spooned eggs onto two plates alongside bacon and toast. They took a seat at the table, he gently took her hand and led them in prayer.

"God please bless this food for its nourishment to our bodies and us to thine service. Amen."

"I love a man that takes the lead and isn't afraid to pray," Amanda remarked with a warm smile.

"Just trust me and I promise I'll never lead you wrong, into danger or heartache. I'll take incredibly good care of you and your heart," Nathan promised as he gently kissed her hand.

CHAPTER FORTY

Pauletta entered her home through the garage. She'd insanely spent the better part of the night outside of Rozalla's bedroom window. After leaving the restaurant, she ignored the restraining order that Haley had taken out and went to their offices. She'd rummaged through files and desk drawers looking for any information should could find on Vince, but Haley had none. All she'd found was a love letter from Scottie. It provided his address, but she determined that it was useless to her. She remembered that Scottie and Vince worked together, but couldn't even find anything with their workplace information.

Finally, she gave up and left. Her first thought was to head home and lick her wounds, but something came over her and before she knew it, she was sitting diagonally across from Rozalla's house waiting for someone to arrive. She figured that once Vince dropped his precious wife off, she'd then have an opportunity to follow him and see where he was staying. They'd arrived, but after waiting forty-five minutes for Vince to come back out of the house, she'd decided to play Peeping Tom. She saw far more than she wanted to.

Everything that she wanted Vince to do to her, he did to Rozalla instead. Pauletta imagined that he was whispering to her, kissing her, inside of her. But the reality was that it was Rozalla getting all the pleasure, leaving her all the pain. The longer she stayed, the harder it became to not smash out that bedroom window and kill his precious Rozalla. All she wanted to do now was sleep. Feeling hurt, rejected, and depressed, Pauletta took to her bed and didn't bother to get out until Monday morning.

With Vince staying over at Rozalla's all night the previous Saturday and with their rekindled relationship, Pauletta could only assume that he'd be moving back in sooner than later. That left her very little time to convince him that she was the better woman. She knew that if she could get him alone, show him that she wasn't desperate or crazy, that he would change his mind and turn his affections towards her. She had to find a way to be alone with him. If only she knew something about Rozalla's work schedule, she'd know when she could lure Vince to her. Then she remembered seeing hospital scrubs and a stethoscope draped over a chair in Rozalla's bedroom. She'd spied it through the window. Pauletta opened her laptop and began to call all of the local hospitals. But facility after facility informed her that they didn't have an employee by that name. Just when she was about to give up, she dialed the number to one of Atlanta's smaller hospitals and hit pay dirt.

"Human Resources, how may I help you?"

"Yes, I need to verify employment for a Mrs. Rozalla Harper," Pauletta chimed in the most pleasant voice she could muster.

"Hold one moment please." The newly hired receptionist buzzed Heather's office to clarify the correct procedure for employment verification. When Heather found out the employee they were wanting information on, she decided to take the call herself.

"Thank you for holding. This is Heather Ramos, how may I help you?"

"Yes, I'm calling to verify employment for Rozalla Harper. Is she employed there?"

"Ma'am I'm sorry, but we don't provide that information over the phone. However, if you fax your request form to

404-333-4433 I'd be glad to fill it out and return it to you," Heather explained.

"So she does work there." Pauletta mumbled.

"I'm sorry ma'am, I didn't hear you."

"Oh, I just said thank you. I'll get that form right over to you."

"Okay, but may I please ask you a question? Is this verification for a new job or credit?"

Pauletta stumbled before coming up with a quick lie. "It's for a credit reference. I'm going to send the fax, but by any chance would you be able to tell me her work schedule?"

"What's really going on, is someone looking for her?" After a long pause, Heather finally continued, "I'm sorry, you don't have to answer that. Mrs. Harper will have to provide you with that information."

"I understand. Thank you for all of your help." Pauletta disconnected the call and rejoiced over the fact that she'd pinpointed Rozalla's place of employment. But she certainly couldn't camp out in front of the hospital for hours on end for Rozalla to show up. There had to be a way to obtain her work schedule. Unless Pauletta read her wrong, there was something in that HR woman's voice that indicated a mix of curiosity and displeasure.

"Maybe she'll give me more information if I show up in person," Pauletta mumbled to herself. With new found determination, she rushed to shower, dressed, and head to the medical center. Pauletta wouldn't rest until she had that schedule and another shot at Vince.

Nervously, Pauletta approached the receptionist's desk and asked for Heather Ramos. She was instructed to have a seat. It took nearly ten minutes for Heather to finally come out and escort the unexpected visitor into her office.

"Have a seat," Heather offered as she motioned to the chairs in front of her desk. "Please don't think me rude, but I have a full day and we didn't have an appointment, so I'd appreciate it if you would make this as brief as possible."

"I completely understand and I promise not to take up much of your time. I called earlier about an employee by the name of Rozalla Harper. I thought maybe I could persuade you to give me her work schedule. We have business, but I've had a hard time catching up with her."

Instead of kicking her out like she should've, Heather let her curiosity and new found contempt for Rozalla get the best of her. "What's your name and what business do the two of you have?"

Stupidly, Pauletta hadn't thought all of this out and began to shift in her seat while trying to concoct a believable lie. She eventually gave up and decided to go with the truth. Something about Heather told her that the truth would serve her better anyway.

"Okay look, my name is Pauletta and I've been having an affair with her husband. Unfortunately, they are trying to work things out, but I know that if I had just a few moments alone with Vince, I could convince him to come back to me. But with them always up under each other, the only shot I have is to approach him when I know that she is nowhere around."

"So does Rozalla know about this little affair?"

"No. He's managed to convince her that we only went out once, but I assure you that's a lie. We were set up by mutual friends, hit it off right away and I'm not ashamed to say that we moved to the bedroom pretty quickly. I understand that they've been together for years, but she screwed up and now it's my turn."

A wicked smile crept across Heather's face. All she could think about was how Rozalla had blamed her for her and Vince's marital problems and ended their friendship. Since Rozalla didn't care about their friendship, Heather decided not to give a damn about her marriage.

"Rozalla works 7:00 am to 7:00 pm Tuesdays, Wednesdays and Thursdays. Vince usually leaves the dealership around 6:00 pm every day. You know he's right there at the big dealership on Buford Highway. You can easily catch him leaving work. Now if you'll excuse me, I have a ton of work. And please understand that if asked, I will deny having ever met you."

"I completely understand. Thank you so much and have a great day." Pauletta practically danced out of the building and to her car. Heather had given her all the information she needed. The rest was up to her.

CHAPTER FORTY-ONE

"Do you guys have any idea how happy I am to see this?" Lisa grinned from ear to ear as she watched her father return his clothes and personal hygiene items to their rightful place. Rozalla had managed to keep his half of the closet empty in anticipation of this day, the day he'd move back in. "Mama, you knew your man was coming back, huh?"

"I prayed, Lisa, I prayed." Rozalla said as she clasped her hands together and smiled with her head raised towards the sky. "I'm so thankful that God is a God of second chances."

"Daddy, I'm thrilled that you're moving back in a lot sooner than you'd planned, but I'm curious as to why. Just last week you two had vowed to date and take things slowly. What happened? Did Mama put that good, good on you?" She giggled like a little kid.

Vince laid a pile of clothes across the foot of the bed and took a deep breath. "Stop being perverted, little girl. At dinner yesterday, Haley told us about that nutcase friend of hers and how she attacked her in their office. Apparently, Pauletta is crazed and has made threats against Haley. Now if she'd attack and threaten her business partner and supposed friend, what would she do to your mama? The woman is obsessed and I thought it best to move back into not only protect Rozalla, but to also send a clear message that I am not available."

"Not that I'm preaching or anything, but just like Mama had to learn a hard lesson, you had your own to learn. Those women out there will never compare to the woman you left behind. Y'all better praise God every single day that He didn't allow your marriage to be permanently destroyed."

"Yes wise one, we have learned our lesson," Rozalla replied. "By the way, where is your sister? I thought she was spending the weekend with you."

"So did I, but when we left here Friday, Ashton called her and you know she went running. That girl dropped me back at my apartment and shot straight down to Athens."

Annoyed, Rozalla sucked her teeth. "Those two have been back and forth for way too long. One week he can't get enough of her and the next he's too busy for her. What really bothers me is how Carmen always makes herself available for him. I don't want my child to be trifled with."

"Who's trifling with you, Lisa?" Vince asked as he brought the last of his things in.

"No one's messing over me. You know that I don't play that. We're talking about your eldest child and that darn Ashton."

"That girl has an incredible mind for business, but gets simple as syrup when it comes to relationships. I used to think that boy was a great catch, but the longer he's around the more I dislike him."

Before another word could be spoken, they heard someone come barreling through the front door of the house. Vince grabbed the bat and headed towards the front door. But as soon as he turned the corner, he dropped the bat and dashed to catch his bloody faced daughter. He swooped Carmen up in his arms and started yelling for help. "Roz, she's hurt bad. Come help me, Baby. Hurry up!"

"Who's hurt?" Rozalla asked as she rounded the corner. When she saw Carmen a panicked scream escaped her mouth. "Oh God, what happened to my baby? Lisa, call nine-one-one."

~~~

The family was huddled in a corner of the medical center's emergency room waiting area praying for Carmen when Amanda arrived. She quietly stepped into the prayer circle and bowed her head. Vince, always the leader and strength of the family turned his child over to God and trusted Him to make her whole and healthy again. "In Jesus name we pray, amen."

"Hey guys, I got here as quickly as I could. What in the world happened?" Amanda asked as she embraced Rozalla.

"We don't know," Rozalla sniffled. "We were at the house talking when we heard her come through the front door. Amanda, she was a bloody mess. I don't know if she was in an accident or what, but I've been begging God to let her be okay."

"I have an idea what happened," Lisa spat. "That damn Ashton, that's what happened!"

"Why would you say that?" Vince asked. "Has he hit her before and if so, why the hell wasn't I told?"

"I'm sorry, Daddy, but she made me swear not to say anything. Anyway, a couple of months ago I went to hang out with her in Athens. While we were at the spa getting massages, Ashton was trying to reach her. Apparently he'd gotten a flat tire and was trying to reach her so that she could come help him out. By the time we finished up and made it to her place, he was there fuming. They got into a heated argument and he slapped her. I jumped in his face and told him I was calling the cops. As soon as I said that he took off and before I could actually call, Carmen grabbed my phone. She said some crap about him not meaning to hit her and not wanting to get him into trouble. And please don't say it because I already know, I should've called anyway."

Vince was livid. He paced the floor, stomping back and forth until anger forced him to lash out and kick a chair across the room. "What kind of punk lays his hands on a female? I don't even understand why he'd be calling her to help with a flat tire. His punk ass needs to learn how to be a man and handle his business on his own. I swear if I saw him right now I'd kill him!"

Rozalla spun around, "Don't say that. God forbid something happen to that jackass and they come looking for you. Lisa, you know better than to make promises like that. You don't ever protect an abuser and you always tell when it's in the best interest of your sister. I'm so disappointed that you didn't say anything. You know better!"

"Cut me some slack, Mama. This family has been a complete mess for the past few months and it all started with you. You should've known better!"

Amanda shook her head in disgust. "All of y'all calm down. Now is not the time to point fingers and place blame. You're just upset about Carmen and understandably so, but sit down and shut up before you all say things you'll regret."

Like children that had been chastised, they did as they were told. Rozalla reached out and took Lisa's hand. Lisa whispered an apology to her mother. And just as everyone got their emotions in check, Heather walked past the waiting room. When she spotted the Harper family, she turned and walked in.

"Sorry, I don't mean to intrude, but may I ask who's hurt?"

Looks of irritation and exasperation immediately spread across everyone's face except for Rozalla's. Although she didn't want to continue a friendship with Heather, she held no ill feelings towards her. Heather only did and said what Rozalla had allowed her to.

Standing to her feet, Rozalla approached Heather with tears in her eyes, "It's Carmen. We don't know what happened to her, all we know is she showed up at the house bloody, bruised, and somewhat incoherent. We're waiting for the doctor to come out now with information on her condition."

"Oh my goodness, I'm so sorry, Roz. Do you want me to check and see what docs are working the ER today and ask for an update?"

"Thanks, but Doctor Rogers is back there and I know he'll take great care of her. Hopefully he'll update us soon. But thanks again."

"No problem. I'll leave you with your family, but if you need anything you know where to find me." Heather gently rubbed Rozalla's arm before walking off.

Returning to her seat, Roz couldn't help but think how nice that was of Heather to check on them despite their last conversation. She wondered if she'd jumped the gun by ending the friendship as opposed to simply setting boundaries. Too bad couldn't she see the spiteful grin that crossed Heather's face or hear the thoughts of *that's what you get* that played in her head as she walked away. It would've removed all doubt as to whether she'd done the right thing or not.

The sight of Dr. Rogers snapped Roz out of thoughts of her broken friendship. "Looking for us, Dr. Rogers?" She asked as she jumped to her feet.

With a warm smile, he approached Roz and her family. "Yes I am and I have some good news for you." Everyone was now standing, staring intently at the doctor, hanging on every word that crossed his lips.

"Roz, your daughter is going to be fine. She's suffered an orbital and nose fracture. She has a couple of bruised ribs, but thankfully none are broken."

A bit confused, Vince asked, "Doctor, what's an orbital fracture?"

"It's a fracture to the eye socket. Luckily, Carmen's isn't bad. I'll prescribe some antibiotics to prevent infection and a steroid to help with the swelling. There was a cut on her cheek that required five stitches. Now she'll be quite sore for a bit, but there's no reason for her to be admitted."

"So we can take her home now?" Roz quizzed.

"Absolutely."

"One last question, Doctor. What most likely caused this kind of trauma to my little girl?" Vince already knew the answer, but wanted to have confirmation from Doctor Rogers.

"I'm sorry, I thought someone had come out to tell you that we'd notified the police. This was physical attack. The police may already be in with her now. Come with me, I'll escort you and Roz to her room so that you hear her statement to the cops."

When Carmen saw her parents come in the room, fresh tears burned her eyes before making their journey down her swollen face. She continued to explain how Ashton had attacked her and dumped her out of the car in front of her parents' house. She didn't know if she was crying more out of feelings of embarrassment or betrayal. It was likely a combination of both. All she knew for sure was that she wanted to go home and rest in the loving arms of her family. She wanted to let their love heal her.

CHAPTER FORTY-TWO

Obsession wouldn't allow Pauletta to stay away from the Harper home. Vince had ignored her text messages and every time she called, he sent her straight to voicemail. For him it was as if she never existed and she was determined to make him remember her, want her, love her.

She knew that Rozalla didn't work on Mondays, but couldn't understand why Vince hadn't shown up at work. She'd waited for him at the dealership until Scottie spotted her. He'd informed her that Vince was with his wife and that she needed to leave and never come back. Pauletta had left the dealership in a huff. She drove straight to Rozalla's only to see Vince carrying in arm loads of clothes. She couldn't believe that he was already moving back in. Consumed by anger, she sped off.

But she was back again, sitting and waiting. She just wanted to catch a glimpse of Vince. She had to see his face. She sat in wait for three hours before spotting Rozalla's car coming down the street with Vince behind the wheel. They were followed closely by Rozalla's flip tongued friend. The heifer that the she blamed for coming between she and Vince in the first place. She watched as everyone exited their cars. A young woman got out of Rozalla's car and ran to unlock the front door while Vince gently lifted another young woman from the back seat of the car. Her arms were wrapped around his neck as he carefully carried her into the house. Of course his wife was following him foot-to-foot like some lovesick puppy dog.

She finally deduced that the young women must've been Vince's daughters. *I bet they'd like me as a stepmother. I'd appreciate their father much more than Rozalla had.* She'd begun to fantasize about what a life with Vince and his daughters would look like. Sunday dinners, shopping with his girls, making love to him. Then violent banging snapped her out of day dream. Amanda was pounding on her car window.

"What the hell are you doing here?" Amanda screamed. "There is nothing or no one here for you, no one wants you here. Now leave before I call the cops, you crazy witch!"

With fire in her eyes, Pauletta started her car slowly pulled away. As she drove down the street, she watched in the rearview mirror as Amanda crossed the street and entered the house. She circled back around, parked a few feet behind Amanda's car and grabbed a box cutter from her glove compartment. It took her less than a minute to slash three of Amanda's tires, jump back in her car and leave.

CHAPTER FORTY-THREE

Carmen had been put to bed in her old room. Rozalla made sure that she had everything she needed and made her as comfortable as possible. While they'd waited for her to be discharged, Lisa had gone to the local pharmacy and gotten Carmen's prescriptions filled. Thankfully so, because as soon as they got home Carmen was in need of a pain pill. Within minutes of going to bed, she was out like a light.

Rozalla returned to the family room only to find Lisa and Amanda begging Vince not to go looking for Ashton. He had the Louisville Slugger in his hand and fire in his eyes. Amanda was standing in front of the door and Lisa was trying to wrangle the bat from his hand. Rozalla walked in and very calmly approached her husband.

"Amanda and Lisa, why don't you guys run out and grab us some dinner. There's some cash in my purse," Rozalla instructed.

"What do you want?" Lisa mumbled.

Amanda took Lisa by the hand as if she were a little kid. "I think you should decide what's for dinner. Let's go."

"Baby, you know that this is not the answer. Besides, the police have a description of Carmen's car, her tag number and Ashton's address. Let them do their job. I know you want to kill him for what he did to our daughter, but that would land you in prison. Is that what you want? To have to watch your back and be always be mindful to not drop the soap?"

"But Roz he put his hands on my girl and then had the nerve to steal her car. Someone needs to teach him a lesson. A hard, painful lesson."

"With these trigger and Taser happy cops, I'm sure his arrest will be a painful one. So let's let them handle it because our family has endured enough and none of us could handle it if you were to get arrested. Besides, Carmen would feel so guilty. Do you really want to put us through that?"

"You know I don't want to cause my angels any heartache, but what kind of father would I be if I let him get away with what he's done?"

"I promise you, he won't get away with this." Rozalla caressed her husband's face. She had to tiptoe to look him eye to eye. "You are a phenomenal father and husband, but you can't continue to be if you're locked up." She kissed him gently and could feel the tension leaving his body.

While Rozalla was calming things down inside, Amanda was outside trying to keep from yelling at the top of her lungs. She couldn't believe that sneaky witch, Pauletta had slashed her tires. That woman was completely out of control and had to be stopped. But calling the cops was useless because it couldn't be proved that she was the one that took a knife to the tires.

"How do you know it was her?" Lisa asked.

"Because she was here when we all pulled up. I spotted her sitting in her car across the street. I waited for everyone to get inside before confronting her. The heifer must have come back after I went inside. And I just bought these tires a week ago."

"I'm going to go get Daddy. He'll know where we can find her and show her what crazy really looks like." Lisa turned towards the house, but Amanda stopped before she could take her second step.

"No, they have enough on their plate right now. Let's wait for AAA to get here and tow the car to Discount Tire. They'll have me up and running in no time."

"Okay, Amanda. Hopefully they'll be here soon and we'll follow them to the shop."

"No, they're waiting on food. I'll ride with the tow truck guy," Amanda advised.

"No the hell you won't. We don't know him and I don't trust anyone that I don't know."

"Lisa, sometimes you have no choice but to trust a stranger. Besides, I have faith that there are still good, honest, kind hearted people in the world. More of them than the evil ones."

"That may be true, but we're not going to take any chances. We've had enough drama and don't need anymore. Especially when it can be prevented," Lisa chided.

A few more minutes passed before the tow truck arrived. The gentleman jumped out of the truck and approached the ladies with a killer smile on his face. And Lisa took note of every pearly white.

"Hello ladies, I'm Evan." He approached them with an outstretched hand.

"Hi Evan, I'm Amanda and this is Lisa. As you can see, someone decided to take their misplaced rage out on my tires."

"Sorry about that. Folks need to learn how to channel life's issues because this is surely not the way. Where would you like for me to tow it?"

"There's a Discount Tires about five miles away," Amanda advised. "That's where I got these so hopefully they'll have mercy and give me a discount."

"Alright, well let me load it up and we'll be on the way. You're welcome to ride in the truck with me if necessary."

Finally breaking her gaze and finding her voice, Lisa interjected. "No, she'll be riding with me. We'll follow you in my car."

Evan flashed those pearly whites again, "Okay Mrs. Lisa, but let me assure you, I'm as harmless as a church mouse."

"Oh, I'm sorry, I didn't mean for that to sound as if I thought you were a danger. And its Ms. I'm quite single."

Both Amanda and Evan chuckled. Lisa's attraction to the five foot eleven inch, caramel coated brother was unmistakable. She didn't mean for her interest to be quite so obvious, but at least he knew and that put the ball squarely in his court.

Amanda was in the tire shop talking with the clerk while Evan unloaded her car from his truck. Lisa conveniently lingered outside in her car until he was finished. He approached her and stooped down beside her open car door.

"Lisa, I'm all done with your friend's car, but before I leave may I ask you a question?"

"Of course, ask away."

"How would you like to accompany me to Kat's Café Friday night? My friend's band is playing and I told him that I'd be there. It's a Jazz band and I must admit, they're pretty good. What do you say?"

"Friday sounds good and Kat's is one of my favorite spots. So I guess that's a yes."

"May I have your number so that I can touch basis with you later in the week?"

"Sure, what's your number? I'll call you and that way we can lock each other's numbers in."

"678-886-6688. I'll be sure and call you in a couple of days." Evan stood to his feet and reached for Lisa hand. She didn't think it was possible for someone to shake her hand both firmly and gently at the same time.

She expected for his hands to be rough from the manual labor, but they were smooth and callus free. "It's been a pleasure meeting you and I look forward to Friday," he said before releasing her hand and taking off in his truck.

Lisa watch him drive away and couldn't help but think *At least something good came of this crappy ass day.*

When Lisa and Amanda finally made it back to the house, Rozalla and Vince questioned them about what took so long to get dinner. Amanda explained what had transpired between her and Pauletta and the damage Pauletta had done to the car. Vince felt horrible and had offered to pay for the new tires. But Amanda had adamantly refused to take his money. She only wanted one thing from Vince and that was Pauletta's address. After swearing that she only wanted it for the purposes of directing the cops to her if anything else happened, Vince caved and gave it to her. Address in hand, Amanda felt that she could now even the playing field.

CHAPTER FORTY-FOUR

It had only taken twenty-four hours for the cops to find and arrest Ashton. Unfortunately, they didn't get him before he'd stripped Carmen's car and sold the parts for drug money. She'd started to see the changes in Ashton months ago, but wasn't sure what to attribute them to. That is until she decided to surprise him with dinner one evening and found his door unlocked and him passed out on the couch with a crack pipe laying on the coffee table.

Carmen was completely in shock. For a moment she thought he might be dead, but when she started screaming and shaking him frantically, he responded by smacking her across the face. That was the first time he'd ever hit her but it certainly hadn't been the last. As she and Rozalla sat at the kitchen table sharing coffee, she recounted the half dozen other times he'd hit her when he was either high or hounding her for money to get high.

"Baby, why didn't you leave him after the first time?" Rozalla asked with confusion etched across her face.

"Mama, I thought I could help him. I honestly thought I could get him over this new found addiction. I know the kind of man he was before he started using drugs and I really wanted to be the one to help him return to his former self." Carmen dropped her head and let her tears fall freely. Rozalla embraced her with the love only a mother could give.

"I know you love who he used to be, but that man is gone. It doesn't matter if he gets clean tomorrow, he'll never be the man you used to know," Rozalla explained. "He'll either choose to stay in the condition he's in or seek help, and get clean. Either way, the decision has to be his. And again, even if he gets clean, he won't be the same because overcoming drug addiction is a lifelong struggle and the experience will make or break him."

"I know all of that, Mama, but I didn't want to just turn my back on him and leave him in his time of need."

"Carmen, you didn't leave him, he left you. He chose drugs over you, over everything. And it will be his choice to stop using. You can't make him stop and to an addict, your love isn't as appealing as his next fix. It's time for you to let him go."

Vince was about to enter the kitchen when he heard Roz talking to their daughter. He decided to stand and listen for a second and his heart broke when he heard Carmen confessing her desire to help Ashton. She was a good girl, but believed too much in fairy tales. He knew that this was a harsh wake up call for her. Finally, he decided to step in the room.

"Is this a private party or can anyone join?"

Carmen eased from her mother's arms and began to wipe her face. "Hey Daddy."

"Hey, sweetie, I thought we'd go look for you a new car today. Are you feeling up to that?"

"Oh my goodness, you're going to buy me a new car?" Carmen asked with a gleam of excitement in her eyes.

"Girl no, you're a successful business woman and capable of buying your own car. However, I am going to give you the down payment so that you can get something nice without a ridiculous monthly payment. How does that sound?"

"That sounds amazing. Especially since I was stupid enough to cough up a nice chunk of my savings trying to help Ashton," Carmen confessed as she dropped her head again.

"You weren't stupid, baby, you were in love," Rozalla said in an effort to ease Carmen's pain.

"Yeah, well I won't be falling in love with anyone else for a very long time. Daddy, thank you so much. Give me twenty minutes and I'll be ready to go."

Rozalla eased up from the table and placed the coffee mugs in the sink. "Do you think getting her a new car is the best thing now? Maybe she needs more time to figure everything out before making financial decisions."

"Roz, I know you want to keep her here and trust me, I'm in no hurry for her to head back to Athens. But physically she's feeling better and last night she asked if she could borrow my truck to go home and check on her salon. She's a grown woman with business to handle. We can't keep her locked up here."

"But it's only been a few days," Roz tried to explain.

"I know, baby, but we can't force, beg or trick her to stay here in her old room. She's grown and with Ashton locked up, I have no fear of her bumping into him."

Roz gave in and went to prepare herself for work while Vince and Carmen went car shopping. By the time she made it back home from the hospital, there was a beautiful new burgundy Maxima parked in the driveway. She knew that this time tomorrow her baby would be back in Athens trying to reclaim her life.

CHAPTER FORTY-FIVE

"Do you really think that this is the best approach?" Nathan asked as he watched people walk the city streets from Amanda's office window. Full of concern, he took slow, deliberate steps across the room before settling into a chair. "She's already slashed your tires. We knew before that incident that she was unstable and now you want to follow her? It sounds like a disaster waiting to happen."

Looking up from her computer, Amanda tilted her head and stared at Nathan as if he had two heads.

"What would you prefer I do? Because what I won't do is sit back and wait for her to do something to Rozalla or Vincent. They are finally getting things back on track, but that idiot is itching for the right moment to attack and ruin it all. I just know she is, I can feel it."

"Which is precisely why I don't want you involved. You'll be the one to get caught in the crossfire. We both know that she won't think twice about destroying anything or anyone that stands between her and Vince." Nathan jumped back up from his seat and began to pace back and forth.

"You're going to walk a hole in my carpet," Amanda teased.

"You're cute, but this isn't funny. I'm going to call an old acquaintance of mine. She has a small private investigation firm. They mostly follow those suspected of infidelity and insurance fraud, but I'm sure she'd be glad to take on your case."

"So is this old acquaintance also an old lover?"

"Why? You jealous?" Nathan asked with a sly grin.

"Stop flattering yourself, I was just curious," she replied as she dropped her head. The last thing she wanted was to come off like some little jealous schoolgirl.

"Yes you are and I like it," he teased. "But no, we never dated. She's actually the ex of one of my homeboys. So what do you say, let's let a professional track little miss crazy."

"Fine, give me her number and I'll set up a meeting with her. If I think she's capable, then I'll gladly let her be the one to keep tabs on Pauletta."

Nathan whipped out his phone and recited the name and number of the investigator to Amanda. "Now that we've got that settled, where are we going for dinner tonight?"

"Who said we were going to dinner? I'm going home, put my feet up and relax. Besides, The Voice is coming on and I don't want to miss it." Truth be told, Amanda rarely watched television, she just wanted to see if Nathan remembered that. She watched as he moved around to her side of the desk. She tried not to giggle when he nibbled on her ear.

"I would've believed you if you'd said you were going home to read, but we both know you don't give a damn about television. So I'll ask again, where are we going for dinner or am I coming over and cooking for you?" he whispered.

Amanda hadn't allowed any real intimacy to occur between them, but she was growing tired of fighting her desires. She wanted to be closer, she wanted to be touched.

"I like a man in an apron," she teased. "Why don't you come over and cook for us while I finish my novel?"

"Sounds like a plan to me." Nathan gave her a gentle peck on the cheek and turned to leave. Just before he opened the door, the turned and said, "I'll be there at seven. Make sure you're wearing something sexy." He gave a wink, opened the door, walked out.

Amanda giggled and wondered, *What have I gotten myself into?* She shook away thoughts of Nathan and their pending dinner plans. It was time to get back to business. She picked up the phone and dialed the number of the investigator.

"Velo Investigations. How may I help you?"

"Yes, may I please speak with Kristen Velo?"

"One moment please."

Amanda tapped her pen on the edge of her desk as she waited for this private investigator to pick up the line. As soon as she started humming along with the music that piped through the phone, Kirsten picked up.

"This is Kirsten, how may I help you?"

"Hi, my name is Amanda Niles and I'm looking to have someone followed."

"Okay Ms. Niles, I'll need a little more information. How bout we set up a meeting? I'll be glad to come to you, if you provide your address and good time for us to meet."

"The sooner the better," Amanda replied. She gave Kristen her work address and had her secretary clear her schedule so that they could meet later that afternoon.

Within the hour Kirsten arrived and was escorted into Amanda's office. Amanda tilted her head to the side and took in every aspect of Kirsten's physical appearance. The woman was not at all what she expected. Kirsten was very much a Plain Jane. Her short, stout stature, crooked wig, and braces had Amanda doing a double take. Although she smiled warmly, her facial expression told the story that her mouth wouldn't dare.

"Hi Kristen, it's so nice to meet you. Please come in and have a seat."

Kirsten waited for the secretary to close the door before speaking. Her sultry voice didn't match the rest of her at all.

"It's nice to meet you as well. But the expression on your face says that I'm not what you were expecting."

"I'm sorry, I didn't mean to look at you strangely. It's just that your voice, well it…"

"Doesn't go with the rest of me, huh?"

"Not exactly," Amanda confessed.

"If you would allow me to, I'd love to peel off some of these layers. It's a tad hot in here."

"Please, help yourself." Amanda's jaw damn near hit the floor as the woman pulled off her wig, removed the fake braces from her mouth and unzipped her dress. Turns out the dress was actually part of a bodysuit that added an additional twenty pounds to Kirsten's frame. Amanda was floored. When all the fakery was pulled off, a lovely, petite, red head stood before her.

"May I take that seat now?" Kirsten asked as she stuffed her disguise into her oversized tote.

"Be my guest," Amanda responded still in awe.
"I'm sorry to have done all of that in front of you, but I came here straight from working a case. And I also wanted you to see how versatile I can be. No one, man nor woman, pays any attention to my alter ego. This costume makes it really easy for me to blend into any crowd or disappear into the background."

"That was incredible and you're hired."

"Well thank you," Kirsten chuckled. Now why don't you tell me about who you want followed, why, and what you expect from me?"

Amanda recounted all of the craziness that Pauletta had done. She shared everything from what had led Vince to date Pauletta in the first place to the crazy woman slashing her tires.

"I know she's going to try something insane and I can't sit around and wait for it to happen. My greatest fear is that she going to attack my friend. Rosetta and Vince have been through so much lately and they don't need crazy ass Pauletta to ruin it all."

"I totally understand." Kirsten obtained Pauletta's home address, explained when and how she would observe Pauletta and alert Amanda of any danger to her or her friends.

Amanda was comfortable and confident in Kirsten's abilities. With that task taken care of, she could already feel the extra stress leaving her body. Now it was time to focus her energies on something more pleasurable. It was time to focus on Nathan.

Her house was always spotless, but that didn't stop Amanda from going home and cleaning as if she were expecting Prince Harry. She checked the clock and realized that she only had an hour before Nathan was due to arrive. Amanda freshened up with a quick shower, and used her new obsession, in shower body lotion, to moisturize before jumping into a cute lounging jumpsuit. Just as she finished applying a little make up and pulling her hair into a ponytail, the doorbell rang. Pleased with her reflection in the full length mirror, she trotted off to let her date in.

"Hey handsome, come on in," Amanda sang as she stepped back to allow him room to enter.

"Hey yourself." Nathan tried hard to hide his appreciation for the way her jumpsuit was fitting, but failed miserably. He gave her the once over, but his eyes stalled on her butt. While Amanda was slim, she still had a curvaceous body that Nathan loved to admire.

She had closed the door and was walking away when she realized that Nathan was still standing in the same spot. "Dude, what are you doing?"

"Just admiring the scenery," he replied as he looked at her lustfully.

Amanda couldn't help but laugh. "While you're being silly I'm starving. Would you and your little grocery bags please come in here and get busy?"

"I'll get busy alright," Nathan mumbled.

"What did you say?"

"Coming dear. Just said that I was coming."

"Liar," Amanda whispered with a chuckle.

Amanda poured a couple of glasses of wine and sat at the bar while Nathan took the salmon, baking potatoes, asparagus, brownie mix, and ice cream out of the bag. They shared small talk as he moved about the kitchen with the ease of a professional chef. She loved how smooth he was. How much swagger and confidence he had. The more time she spent with him the sexier he got. A man that could cook, was successful professionally, and offered stimulating conversation was every girl's dream. Or at least he was hers. She was more and more convinced of it with the passing of each day.

"Madam, may I offer you our house special featuring honey chipotle salmon?" Nathan placed their plates on the table and refilled their wine glasses. "Take a bite and tell me what you think," he instructed as he sat across from her.

"Oh my goodness, Nathan, this is delicious. Where did you learn to cook?"

"My mom. She used to tell me that she refused to have a son that had to depend on a woman for a home cooked meal. She made sure that my brother and I knew how to cook, do laundry, and properly clean a house."

"Tell her I said thank you," Amanda teased.

Nathan loved seeing her enjoy his food. In all honesty, he enjoyed everything about her. He hadn't felt so connected to a woman in a long time and knew that falling deeply in love with her was inevitable.

They laughed, talked, and ate until their plates were clean. "You ready for dessert?"

"Those brownies do smell good," Amanda said, but the look on her face said that the brownies weren't necessarily the dessert she wanted.

Hoping that he wasn't misreading the signs, Nathan got up, moved around the table and took Amanda's hand. He gently pulled her up from her seat and gazed into her eyes. He was looking for anything, any sign that might have suggested she wanted him step off, but there was none. He placed his hand on the side of her face and leaned in for a kiss. One small kiss turned into another more passionate kiss. Their intensity continued to grow until they were both panting lustfully.

"I want you so badly," Nathan moaned.

Without speaking a word, Amanda led him to her bedroom. She could tell that he wanted to rip the clothes from her body, but loved that he chose to operate with a slow hand. He slowly kissed her mouth, neck, breasts as he removed her clothes. He didn't savagely toss her on the bed, but laid her down with a seductive authority. He kissed, licked, and teased every inch of her body until she was ready to explode. But when he entered her, she gasped. He filled her up and moved in a way that she hadn't experienced. Her body responded with an orgasmic burst that in turn took his breath away. They moved and moaned until they collapsed in a tangled heap of complete satisfaction.

CHAPTER FORTY-SIX

Frustration had been ruling Pauletta's world. She'd been staking out Rozalla and Vince's home, but was unsuccessful at catching Vince alone. That idiot wife of his only left his side to go to work and apparently his daughters had no life. One of them was always with him. She'd tried going to his job, but when he refused to see her she caused a bit of a scene and ended up being escorted from the dealership by security. However, Pauletta was not one to easily give up. She was once again parked diagonally across the street from the Harper's house. Neither of the girls cars were there and Rozalla was supposed to be at work in an hour. Pauletta had her bottled water and romance novel, she was completely ready to patiently wait for Rozalla to leave. As she reclined her car seat she noticed the frumpy woman driving down the street. They briefly locked eyes as the woman passed by. Pauletta never realized that the woman simply circled the block and parked several yards behind her.

While Pauletta waited for her chance to get Vince alone, Kirsten was busy working. She'd called her friend who just happened to be a detective for the Atlanta Police Department. Before he could even say hello, she chimed, "Hello my delightful detective."

"Oh gracious. Hi Kirsten, what do you need?"

"Okay, I'm a little offended. What makes you think I want something?"

"Girl, we've been friends for as long as I can remember. I know you better than you know yourself and I definitely know when you want something. So spit it out. Who are you tailing now?"

"Well since you asked, you could save me a lot of time by giving me the rundown on this woman named Pauletta M. Hines."

"Give me a second." Detective Charles Payne had been with the department for eight years. There was always something to investigate, but regardless of how busy he was, he always took the time to help Kirsten.

"Is this woman a doctor?"

"Yes, she's a psychiatrist or psychologist, some kind of head doctor. Did you find anything?"

"Her record seems to indicate that she's in need of a head doctor. Apparently she's not one to take no for an answer. She's never served any real time, but has been arrested for stalking, trespassing, and simple assault."

"Why the hell hasn't she been locked up?" Kirsten demanded.

"Girl, don't raise your voice at me," Charles teased.

"She's got a habit of pleading no contest. She did serve three months in county lock up on the assault charge, but was given community service and fined for the others. I also see that another psychiatrist has filed a restraining order against her."

"Yes, that was actually her business partner. This Pauletta woman has become obsessed with a man she went out with a couple times. When he decided to go back to his wife, she went ballistic. Started stalking him, attacked her business partner. She's a real nut case."

"She sounds crazy as hell. I know you have a job to do, but please be careful."

"You worried about me, Sexual Chocolate?" Kirsten teased.

"You're so silly," Charles laughed. "But yes, she sounds like the kind of criminal that will escalate to more violent crimes. Seriously, be careful."

"I promise I will. And thanks for the information. I'll touch bases with you in a day or two."

As soon as she disconnected her call, Kirsten noticed a woman leaving the Harper house in what looked like nursing scrubs. *That must be the wife*, she thought to herself. She also noticed Pauletta peeking over the steering wheel with her eyes fixed on the woman. Pauletta watched intently as the woman pulled out of the driveway and drove down the street. As soon as the woman was out of eyeshot, Pauletta jumped out of her car and headed for the house. Kristen had her camera out with its zoom lens attached. She had snapped a few pictures of Pauletta peeking in the windows and preparing to knock on the door when another car rolled down the street and pulled into the driveway. Kristen continued taking pictures as the madness unfolded.

Haley and Scottie jumped out of a SUV, approached Pauletta, and the shouting began.

"What the hell are you doing here?" Haley demanded. "You know what, it doesn't even matter, just leave!" She screamed before giving Pauletta a chance to answer.

"Are you the police now? This isn't your house, you can't make me leave," Pauletta snapped back.

"Watch me, you crazy bitch." Haley pulled out her cell phone to call 911, but was stunned when Pauletta knocked the phone from her hand. Immediately, Scottie stepped between the two women.

"Put your hands on her again or her property and I will beat your crazy ass myself," Scottie warned.

Pauletta's eyes grew wide as she started screaming at the top of her lungs and slapping herself in the face. "No, please stop. You're hurting me. Someone please get him off of me," she cried as she threw her body against a post on the front porch. All of the commotion drew Vince out to the front porch just in time to see Pauletta abusing herself. Without hesitation he dialed 911. He stood there in complete shock as Pauletta began flailing her body against Scottie. Her screams pierced the quiet of the neighborhood and drew neighbors out in time to witness what looked like a man and woman beating on another woman. Pauletta was relentless as she bounced her body between Scottie and Haley. They tried to hold her, tried to push her off of them, but from afar it looked as if they were knocking her around.

Vince finally snapped out of his trance and was able to wrap Pauletta up in a bear hug. He sat her down in a porch chair in an attempt to put space between her and the others.

"See Vince, I knew you still wanted me. You don't protect people you don't want or don't care about," Pauletta sobbed.

"Pauletta, there is not enough money in the world to make me want you. I'm back with my wife and you need to accept that. The police are on their way here. Maybe they can take you to a facility where you can get the help that you desperately need. Your mind isn't right and I will not tolerate you coming around me, my family or my friends. Get it through your head woman, I don't want you!" Vince barked.

Pauletta had the devil in her eyes. "Before it's all over you'll be begging for me," she warned. As police sirens blared on their approach to the house, she took off running to her car. She was gone before the cop could throw his car in park.

Kristen sat with her mouth gapped open. She'd never witnessed anyone so insane. Suddenly she snapped out of her sense of shock, dropped her camera, and took off behind Pauletta. Unfortunately, her hesitation caused her to lose track of Pauletta. Kirsten didn't see her anywhere.

Instinctively, she called her client, Amanda.

"Hi Kirsten, is everything okay?"

"Not exactly. Pauletta just sped away from the Harper's home after causing an insane scene. She was driving so fast that I lost her. I wanted to put you on alert as she is incredibly irritated and I don't know what she may do next. I'm hoping that she has simply decided to go home and cool off."

"What kind of scene?" Amanda asked in a panic.

"I'll fill you in on all the details later. I just wanted you to be aware and to pay close attention to your surroundings. I'm headed over to her residence to see if she's there. If she's not, my next stop will be the hospital where your friend works. I'll keep you posted."

CHAPTER FORTY-SEVEN

Lisa had headed out early to spend the day with Evan. He'd turned out to be a really good guy. She didn't know if it was in the cards for them to become a serious couple, but they were certainly enjoying their time with one another. She was on a high from the day's activities, in a mood so joyful that she didn't think anything could destroy it. That is until she entered her parents' house and heard the conversation that was taking place. Her mom, dad, Amanda, Haley, and Scottie were all speaking with voices full of concern and anger.

"Roz, I'm so sorry that you had to come in from a long day's work to this foolishness. I should've trusted what we had and saw past your mistakes. If I had none of this would be happening," Vince said.

"No, I'm the one that's sorry," Haley blurted out. "I'm the one that brought this crazed lunatic into your lives. I can't believe I ever trusted her, ever believed that she would always do what was in the best interest of my friends. I don't even know how her crazy ass got a license to practice."

"Let's be honest guys. If I'd acted like the wife I was supposed to, if I treated my husband with the same love he's always treated me with all of this would've been avoided. Me and my foolish ways are to blame and I accept that, I own it," Roz sniffled as tears strolled down her face.

Vince stepped towards her to offer comfort when she suddenly took a step back and raised her finger.

"But if that bitch thinks she's going to ruin to my family and take my husband, she's got another thought coming."

Lisa stepped further into the family room. "What's going on? What happened?"

"Come on in and have a seat, baby girl," Vince instructed. He shook his head in disgust as he recounted the events of the day for his youngest daughter. He explained how Pauletta had been stalking them. How she beat herself while throwing her body against Haley and Scotti. The look on Lisa's face was the same shocked look that had covered Rozalla's when they recounted the events for her.

"Daddy, I don't mean to be disrespectful, but did you sleep with her? I mean did you two have any kind of sexual involvement? I only ask because this seems to be the behavior of a woman that gave herself to a man that rejected her. Not just rejected her advanced, but rejected her after he'd had her."

Vince dropped his head and tried to keep from making eye contact with Roz. He could feel her stare and that of his daughter burning holes through him. His prolonged silence pretty much answered the question, but he knew he still had to speak up and tell the truth.

"I swear I never meant for anything to happen." He glanced at Roz and see tears forming in her eyes.

"I never touched her in a romantic way and when she offered herself to me I told her no. As I was trying to leave her house, she started unbuckling my pants, I told her no, tried to push her away. But she dropped to her knees and my body betrayed me. I was weak. When she was done, she again tried to get me to stay, but I told her that I wasn't interested in her that way and I left." He could see the disappointment in Lisa's eyes and the pain in Roz's as she wiped the tears that stained her face. Vince was so ashamed, but he'd said the truth in front of everyone and felt a slight sense of relief as the fear of his dirty little secret melted away.

"Roz, I am so sorry. I swear I never meant for anything like that to happen. I shouldn't have allowed it to happen." He approached Roz with outstretched arms only to be greeted with a powerful slap across the face.

"I acted a fool, I know that, but I never cheated on you. I would never have allowed another man to get close enough to even tempt me. You betrayed our vows, Vince, you betrayed our marriage." Roz wiped her tears, turned and left the room.

Vince started to go after Roz, but Amanda stopped him. "Vince, it might be better if you give her little time. Let me go talk to her," she said as she stood to her feet and slowly headed down the hall.

He dropped to the sofa with his head in his hands. Scottie nor Haley spoke a word. They waited for his daughter to comfort him, to tell him that she understood. But Lisa had no sympathy for her father. She couldn't bring herself to look at Vince let alone comfort him. Instead, she picked up her purse and headed back to her old room to wait for an opportunity to speak with her mother.

"Look man, it's going to be okay. Roz just needs a little time to digest everything. This idiot running around and now this, it's a lot to take in, but she loves you. You guys have reconnected in a way that neither of you imagined you could. She's not going to walk away now. And you saw her earlier, there's no way in hell that she's going to let Pauletta win this battle.

Haley stood to her feet and grabbed her purse. "He's right you know. This is a little stumbling block, but you two will get past it." She patted him on the shoulder in an attempt to lend support. "But for now we're going to head out and give you all a chance to decompress and regain focus." Haley reached for Scottie's hand before turning and walking towards the door.

Vince was left with only his thoughts and a heart full of regret.

CHAPTER FORTY-EIGHT

Pauletta had been pacing back and forth all night. She was constantly from the kitchen to the front window. She hadn't noticed the car following her earlier, but she'd noticed it when she'd gone out to check the mail. A little while later when she peeked out it was still there. She'd grabbed her binoculars to get a better look at the driver. She didn't know the less than average looking woman, but somehow she seemed familiar.

One thing was for sure, Pauletta knew that she didn't belong there. Living on a quiet street, knowing her neighbors and the cars they drove left no doubt in her mind that this stranger was up to no good. Not to mention that every time she looked out the window, the woman seemed to be looking at her. The car had left earlier, but returned about fifteen minutes later and parked on the curb of the cross street, but still facing Pauletta's house. The windows were tinted, but seeing through the windshield was no problem.

Wine glass in hand, Pauletta walked back to the window and that's when it hit her. That was the woman that passed her at Vince's house. Had he hired someone to follow her? The thought of it sent Pauletta into a rage. *These fools want to play games with me. Oh I've got a game for their asses*, she thought to herself. She went and poured the last of the wine into her glass and headed back to the window, but this time the car was gone. It was the last time she'd see that car for the night. The rising of the sun found Pauletta working on a plan to get her man and get rid of everyone else. Meanwhile, Kirsten was sitting in Amanda's kitchen sharing information with her over coffee.

"Your friends need to go to the police immediately and file for restraining orders. Seriously, not just Vince, but his wife and especially the friends that she was throwing herself against. I've seen that done before, it's the perfect set up for her to try and file assault charges against them," Kirsten explained.

"You've got to be kidding! They told me about the incident, but was it really that insane?"

Kirsten opened her laptop and showed Amanda the pictures she'd taken. She then unlocked her phone and played Amanda the snippet of video footage she'd managed to capture.

"Damn, I guess she is that insane," Amanda remarked.

"I stayed on her until late last night. After she left the Harper's house, she went home and that's where she stayed. I left for a brief moment because I thought I saw her look out the window. But after circling the block a couple of time, I parked on an adjacent street and didn't leave again until after eleven o'clock."

"Thanks so much, Kirsten, you're doing an amazing job. But tell me, how can I get a copy of the pictures and video? I mean that valuable proof that they'll need to file for that restraining order."

Kirsten reached in her bag and pulled out a flash drive. "Here you go. Everything is on there." She stood to her feet and gathered her things.

"Thanks for the coffee. I'm going to swing back by Pauletta's to see if she's still there, then I'm heading to the Harper's place and set up. I think we'll be better served if I see her coming versus trying to catch her."

"Sounds good. I'll reach out to you a little later to see if anything new develops," Amanda advised as she escorted Kirsten to the door. To her surprise, Nathan was on the other side of the door preparing to knock.

"Good morning, beautiful," he said flashing that killer smile.

"Good morning. Nathan, you remember Kirsten, the private detective you told me about." The two exchanged pleasantries before Kirsten took off. Amanda turned her full attention to Nathan.

"To what do I owe this pleasure?"

Nathan raised a bag from Amanda's favorite bakery. "I thought you might enjoy a fresh, cinnamon raisin bagel. We could brew some coffee, share some food, and whatever else might come to mind."

Amanda took the bag and peeked inside. "Why didn't you tell me about the donuts?"

"Those are to cure my sweet tooth in case you don't let me nibble on you," Nathan winked.

Amanda burst into laughter. "Man, get your corny butt in here and don't ever let me hear you say anything that lame again." She led the way to the kitchen, grabbed a couple of plates and filled another coffee cup. They sat at the table where they ate and talked. Amanda filled Nathan in on everything that had transpired the previous day. She retrieved her laptop so that she could show him everything that Kirsten had shared with her. Just like her, Nathan was shocked by Pauletta's wild behavior.

"So what now?" he asked.

"Now I take my butt over to their house and show them all of this. They need to head to the police department as soon as possible to try and apply for a restraining order."

"Well let me get out of your hair," Nathan said as he started to stand.

"I was hoping you'd come with me. I won't be there long and then we could enjoy the rest of the day together."

"Sounds like a plan to me, but do we have to leave right now?" Nathan asked with a seductive grin.

Amanda leaned in for a kiss. "They can wait another hour or two."

CHAPTER FORTY-NINE

The sound of the front door slowly creaking open freaked Rozalla out. Vince had just left to run a quick errand and Lisa was in her old room sleeping. Her mind immediately went to Pauletta. She grabbed the Louisville slugger and braced herself against the wall, ready to knock the intruders head off. As the footsteps got closer, Rozalla readied herself and swung. The bat hit the door frame and Carmen fell backwards and hit the floor.

"What the hell is going on? Am I going to be attacked with that damn bat every time I come over here?" Carmen spat.

"Baby, I'm so sorry. Are you okay? Did I hit you?"

"I should've stayed my ass at home," Carmen grumbled as she stood to her feet.

"Did I hit you?" Rozalla asked again as she dropped her weapon and tried to help her daughter up.

"No, but you tore the hell out of the door frame. I'm sure Dad will be happy about that. Where is he anyway and what has you so scared?"

"Come on in the kitchen and let me get you some coffee. Are you hungry?"

"I am," Lisa interjected as she lazily walked into the kitchen. "And feeding me is the least you can do after waking me up with all that banging and screaming."

Carmen grabbed a bottle of water from the refrigerator. "Can one of y'all just tell me where Dad is and what has this one over here so damn jumpy?" she quizzed as she nodded her head in her mom's direction.

Lisa sat across from Carmen and filled her in on everything that was going on. Since her incident with Ashton and returning home to Athens, Carmen had been out of the loop when it came to all the family drama. She'd been too busy dealing with her own drama. Two days after returning home, she learned that Ashton's mom had bailed him out. It didn't take him long to start harassing Carmen with phone calls and unexpected visits.

Despite the restraining order, he'd bang on her door all times of night. He'd drop by her salon, but would always leave before the police could arrive. He'd become great at avoiding the cops and even better at harassing her. She'd come to her parents' house to seek help from her dad, maybe crash with them for a few days just to get a break from Ashton's craziness, but they clearly had enough going on without her adding to the mess.

"I can't believe Daddy let that woman perform oral sex on him." Carmen's disgust for her father's lack of judgement and self-control was evident on her face and in her voice.

"So now we have an unstable woman who is being fueled by lust and rejection. If that's not an explosion waiting to happen I don't know what is."

"Enough about that," Rozalla said as she sat down with a cup of coffee. "What brings you up from Athens?"

Carmen contemplated if she should share her craziness, but decided to go with her first thought and keep it to herself. Her mom didn't need anything else to worry about. "Nothing really, just wanted to catch up with you guys. So tell me,

Mama, what does this revelation about Daddy, mean for you two's relationship, your marriage?"

Rozalla ran her hands through her hair in frustration. "As angry as I want to be, I can't bring myself to feel that way. I can't help but feel that I brought this on myself. I pushed him away with all of my foolishness, selfishness, and unrealistic demands. We were perfectly happy until I ruined it, so I guess this is my payback."

"No it's not. Babe, I never wanted to hurt you and when I went out with that woman it was not done as a way to cause you pain or as payback. My only intention was to be her friend, someone to occasionally hang out with. Dating wasn't on my radar and I should've made sure that it wasn't on hers either," Vince explained as he walked further into the kitchen. They were so lost in conversation that they hadn't heard him come through the side garage door.

"I am so sorry. I'm sorry for not being stronger, for thinking that the company of another woman was worth turning my back on you," he said kneeling in front of Rozalla.

Tears rolled down Rozalla's cheeks as her husband rested his head in her lap. "We both fell short. I didn't appreciate all that we'd built, all that you'd been to me and in return, you no longer trusted me. You lost faith in us. But now we know better. It's time for us to both forgive and forget. We've got dragons to slay and a happy life to return to. We now know better and we will do better," she tearfully spoke as she gently rubbed his back.

By the time she finished talking, the entire family was in tears. They were cleansing, renewing, and restoring tears that gave them comfort in knowing that as a family they were headed in the right direction. It was a beautiful moment until the silence was shattered by the violent pounding on the front door.

"I know you're in there Carmen. You can't get away from me that easily. You've got to drive more than a few miles to lose me, baby girl. I'm not going anywhere that easily, you ain't gonna shake me, girl."

Vince jumped to his feet. "Is that Ashton?" he asked as he rushed towards the door.

"Call the cops!" He yanked the door open and snatched Ashton up by the collar.

"What the hell are you doing banging on my door and stalking my daughter?"

"Let me go, man," Ashton yelled as he yanked himself from Vince's grip. "I just want to talk to Carmen. All I want is five minutes of her time."

"That crack, meth or whatever you're on has clearly killed every brain cell you had. She doesn't want you, not now, not ever and you're in violation of a restraining order. The cops are on their way here now, you dumb ass."

That statement seemed to sober Ashton up real quick and he took off running. As he took off down the block, Pauletta started her rental car and took off behind him. She'd waited until 1:00 am, when it was clear that Kirsten had left for the night, and took off for the airport. She rented a small compact car and headed straight to Vince's neighborhood. She'd been trying to figure out how she could get Vince alone and felt that the character running away from the house just might be her answer.

CHAPTER FIFTY

Kirsten was at a loss. She'd been to Pauletta's house, but there was no sign of her. She'd driven by the Harper's house several times, but didn't see her car or any car for that matter, parked on the street. She was starting to panic, how had she lost her target, what would she tell her client? Whatever she was going to say to Amanda, she had to come up with it quickly because Amanda and Nathan had just pulled into the Harper's driveway.

Kirsten decided to drive around one more time before speaking with Amanda. She'd covered almost a two block radius before she spotted Pauletta talking to some guy on a corner. Keeping her distance, she pulled over to the side of the road, grabbed her binoculars and watched. She saw Pauletta pull money out of her pocket and offer it to the man who happily accepted. She could see the man shaking his head no, but shortly after he slid into the passenger seat of the car and the pair drove away. She followed them and was surprised to see Pauletta circle back around, pull into the carport of a house adjacent to the Harper's and let herself in. No wonder Kirsten hadn't been able to find her, who would've thought to look in that house.

Kirsten couldn't figure out how Pauletta had gained access to the house. Where were the people that lived there? She whipped out her phone and called her assistant.

"Hi boss lady, what can I do for you?"

"Hey Ann. Do me a favor and look up 2177 Springleaf Drive in the realtor database and tell me what you find."

After a few keystrokes, Ann was able to give her all the information she needed. "That house is now owned and maintained by SunTrust Bank. Looks like it went into foreclosure and was vacated about three months ago."

"Well that explains how this crazy ass woman was able to break in without detection. Thanks Ann, I'll check back in after a while." Kirsten disconnected the call and immediately dialed Charles' number.

"Hey woman, what you need?"

"Hello my favorite detective, how are you?"

"Oh hell, it must be a big favor, you're already trying to butter me up."

"It just requires a little manpower." Kirsten went on to explain the situation and wanted Charles to get a couple of uniformed officers to arrest Pauletta and her little friend for breaking and entering."

"Oh sweetie, you're asking a lot. You don't see any evidence of a break in, no windows are broken, nothing looks out of order—"

"Nevermind, Charles, it looks like they're leaving. I'm going to trail them and see what they're up to."

"Please be careful, Kirsten."

"I will and I promise to check in with you a little later on." Kirsten disconnected the call as she eased away from curb and began to follow Pauletta.

They drove the city streets until Pauletta had maneuvered her way to one of the roughest areas of town. Kirsten didn't understand what Pauletta could possibly be doing winding up, down, and around the drug infested neighborhood. Then she saw her pull up to a curb and holler out the window at a young man standing on a corner.

He approached her car, took a fist full of dollars from her and then passed her a little plastic bag. *Humph, drug deal*, Kirsten thought to herself. She once again eased away from the curb and followed Pauletta. But this time, without realizing it, she followed her right down a long, dead end alley. Kirsten kept her distance, but couldn't throw her car into reverse fast enough when she suddenly realized that Pauletta's passenger had jumped out of the car and was running towards her with his gun drawn.

"Oh God, help me Lord, spare me," she prayed as she put the car in gear and hit the gas. But it was too late, she couldn't outrun the bullets. One flew straight through the windshield and into Kirsten's chest. She slumped over the steering wheel as her car continued to roll backwards until it hit a passing car. People began to rush towards Kirsten's car as Pauletta sped away, leaving the shooter to fend for himself.

As people gathered and tried to open her locked doors, Kirsten managed to hit redial on her phone.

"Hey, woman."

"Charles, they shot me. It burns—"

"Kirsten, who shot you? Where are you? Kirsten, Kirsten!"

"That bitch got what she deserved," Pauletta sang as she whipped the rental car into the carport. She walked into the abandoned house as if she owned it. She was so pleased with herself that she popped open a bottle of wine, plopped onto the pile of blankets that covered the floor and toasted to her accomplishment.

"I toast to me and my brilliance. One bitch down and three more to go. Once I get Haley, that Amanda chick, and Rozalla out of the picture, Vince will be all mine."

CHAPTER FIFTY-ONE

Amanda was literally shaking with fear as she and Nathan pulled up to Rozalla's house. She'd received a phone call from Kirsten's assistant who advised her of the shooting. At this point she didn't know if Kirsten was dead or alive, all she knew was that she'd been shot and they had one of the assailants in custody. Apparently, they found him in an abandoned building near the crime scene high on meth. They were still trying to locate the driver of the car.

"Hey there," Rozalla sang cheerfully when she opened the door. It only took a few seconds for her to realize that something was very wrong. Anguish covered Amanda's face.

"Come on in the kitchen and let me get you some water while you tell me what's wrong," Rozalla instructed as she led the way.

Vince stood to greet their guests, but quickly realized there that this wasn't just another social visit. "What's up, Nathan? Hey Amanda, what's going on?" He asked as he offered a handshake and a hug. He pulled out a seat for Amanda while Roz offered them water or coffee.

"I don't want anything to drink, Roz. I just need you two to have a seat and listen," Amanda pleaded.

Roz and Vince stopped what they were doing and did as Amanda asked. They all sat around the table and anxiously waited for her to speak.

"I first need to apologize to the two of you. I caught that crazy ass Pauletta watching you all's house a little while back. I confronted her and in turn she slit my tires. I know I should've told y'all, but things were already so crazy and I didn't want to add more problems to an already strained situation."

"You're right, you should've told us," Vince chided.

"I know and again, I'm sorry. But I did take measures to make sure you all were protected, at least that was my intent. I hired a private detective to keep an eye on Pauletta and make sure that she didn't do anything crazy. Unfortunately, the detective was shot. I know that Pauletta is behind this," Amanda began to sob. "I don't know her condition. All I know is that they've arrested the shooter, but not the driver he was with."

"Oh my Lord!" Rozalla dropped her head in disbelief. "I can't believe she's this crazy. Trying to kill people. What's to stop her from coming here to kill us next?"

Vince moved towards his wife to try and comfort her, but the sound of someone banging on the door stopped him cold. He jumped from his seat and headed to the front door. Vince was ready to attack Pauletta, but it was Scottie and Haley that stood before him instead.

"What are you two doing here?"

"We saw the news and came right over. We wanted to make sure that you all were okay," Scottie explained.

"Why wouldn't we be okay?"

"Man, y'all need to turn the television on. There's been a shooting and the cops are looking for Pauletta. They think she was behind it."

"Come on in and lock the door." Vince called out for everyone else to join them in the family room as he turned the television to Channel 2 Action News.

They were all stunned to see that the shooter was none other than Ashton. How had he allowed himself to sink so low? The police did not give the condition of the victim, but did say that there was a massive manhunt for Pauletta. They had searched her home, but had not yet found her. As the news anchor began to give background information on Pauletta, the sound of sirens pulled everyone's attention away from the television.

Vince jumped up and ran to the window as a SWAT truck and three cop cars ascended on a vacant house diagonally across from theirs.

"What's going on, Vince?" Rozalla asked as they all scrambled to see out of the front windows.

They all watched in amazement as the police burst into the house. They were only in there for a few minutes before they poured back out into the street. Apparently their search came up empty. One of the men with the officers trotted across the street. Vince swung the door open before he had a chance to knock.

"Good afternoon everyone, I'm Detective Charles Payne. Do you mind if I come in for a minute?"

Vince stepped aside and allowed the detective to enter. They all took a seat, anxiously waiting to hear what he had to say. They were in shock as they learned of Pauletta moving into the abandoned house and bribing Ashton with drugs to get him to kill Kirsten. Rozalla cried as the detective advised them that their lives could very well be in danger. She looked at Vince with a combination of love and disgust. Yes, she'd made a mistake, but nothing she'd done or said to Vince warranted this kind of retaliation. She couldn't believe the insanity that her husband had invited into their lives.

CHAPTER FIFTY-TWO

Detective Payne promised to keep them informed on their search for Pauletta and assured them that their neighborhood would be patrolled every half hour. The other officers had collected the items Pauletta had left in the house for evidence and began pulling away one by one. Vince took Rozalla by the hand and led her back to the family room.

"Since we're all hunkered down here, can I get you guys something to eat?" Rozalla offered as their friends followed them back through the house.

"Good idea, babe, I'll help you throw something together," Vince offered. They were headed towards the kitchen when there was another knock at the door.

"Go ahead guys, I'll get it," Amanda offered. "Maybe they've found that crazy ass Pauletta." So sure that it was an officer, Amanda unlocked the door and threw it open without first looking to see who it was. To her horror, Pauletta was standing there in sunglasses and holding a gun.

"Say one word and I'll blow your brains out," Pauletta warned. Now step back, close and lock the door." She held the gun with both hands, finger on the trigger as she stepped inside and watched Amanda follow her instructions. "Now lead the way. Take me to wherever my man is."

"You've got to know that the cops are looking for you. Do yourself a favor and turn yourself in. This is only going to get you in more trouble."

"Bitch I didn't ask you for your legal advice. Now shut up and take me to Vince."

"Who is it, Amanda?" Vince asked as he rounded the corner.

"Hi, Handsome."

"Pauletta, what are you doing? Put the gun down before you hurt somebody," he demanded.

"I will put the gun down once we are far away from here. I came to get you. This is our opportunity to start over, to be together without all of these distractions," she said as her eyes narrowed towards Rozalla when she stepped into the room. "Are you ready to say your goodbyes, Mrs. Harper?"

Tears began to roll down Rozalla's face. "Please don't hurt him."

"Hurt him? Girl please, I'm giving you the opportunity to say goodbye because I'm going to kill you," she laughed wickedly.

"How did you get in here and why do you want me dead?" Rozalla sobbed.

"Well, I hung out in the backseat of your car until all the cops left and then your friend here was kind enough to let me in. You might want to check that peep hole next time," she giggled at Amanda. "Now tell me, who else is here?"

Rozalla lowered her head and cut her eyes down the hall trying to signal for Scottie, Haley and Nathan to be quiet and ease out the back. "No one, it's just us three."

"You lying bitch!" Pauletta screamed as she started shaking the gun in Rozalla's direction. "I saw all your little friends as they filed in here. All of y'all get your asses out here before I shoot this heifer!" she screamed.

Nathan led the trio into the living room. His heart broke as he looked into Amanda's eyes. He could see her fear and hated the feeling of helplessness that hung over him like a wet blanket over a campfire. He tried to move closer to her, but was quickly stopped by Pauletta.

"That's far enough, Romeo. Stay over there with the rest of your little friends."

As Pauletta barked instructions, movement outside of the front window caught Rozalla's eye. Realizing that help had arrived, she tried to remain expressionless and dart her eyes away from who she hoped would save them.

"What the hell are you looking at? Who's out there?" Pauletta asked as she spun around to try and see whom or what Rozalla saw. But there was no one there. All she saw was the neighborhood she'd come to know so well. A patrol car was making its way down the street, but she wasn't concerned by their slow, leisurely drive.

"Close the blinds," she said to Vince as she motioned towards him with the gun.

Vince went to the window and started closing the blinds. He was shocked to see Lisa standing to the side of the house with the cell phone to her ear. Knowing that help was on the way, he breathed a sigh of relief, closed the blinds and took his place by Rozalla's side.

"Why do you keep going back to her, Vince? Don't you see all that I've done for you, all that I'm doing so that we can be together? Do you see me at all?" Pauletta's eyes welled up with tears as she waiting for Vince to reply. She wanted him to come to her side, to show her that he wanted to be with her. More than anything she wanted to see him turn away from Rozalla, to reject her. "Answer me dammit!"

"Pauletta, I could lie to you and tell you everything you want to hear. But the truth is that I love my wife. I've always loved her and she's the only woman I'll ever want. I tried to tell you over and over again that I wasn't looking for a new relationship. You knew I was still married. Yes, we were going through a rough patch, but this woman is my heart."

Without saying another word, Pauletta pointed the gun at Rozalla and pulled the trigger.

"Oh God!" Rozalla screamed when she hit the floor and realized that Vince had pushed her out the way and taken the bullet for her. "What have you done?" she screamed at Pauletta. "Vince, baby please don't leave me," Roz sobbed as she saw the blood gushing from his shoulder. "Somebody get me some towels," she shouted, but the house was in complete chaos with everyone screaming and Pauletta swinging the gun around, pointing it from person to person. "Get me some towels now, dammit! Get them now!" she managed to scream over all the noise.

Amanda didn't wait for permission to move, she took off to the bathroom as Pauletta screamed after her. It only took a few seconds for her to return with an armful of towels. She knelt down beside Rozalla and Vince and started passing Roz towels.

As everyone started moving towards Vince and screaming for an ambulance, Pauletta felt all control of the situation slipping through her fingers. Out of desperation, she shot a bullet through the ceiling. The loud pop caused everyone to jump and a dead silence to fall over the room.

"I want all of you to go back to the master bedroom right now!" she barked. "If I have to say it again, someone is going to die, now move. Move quickly."

Nathan and Scottie escorted Haley and Amanda to the back bedroom. Pauletta followed closely with the gun trained at the back of Nathan's head. She'd ordered Rozalla to not move from Vince's side. Once the others were in the bedroom, she ordered them into the closet, took their cell phones, and locked the closet door. The sound of sirens sent her into more of a panic. Pauletta took off to the front of the house, but as she rounded the corner she was smacked in the face with the infamous Louisville slugger. The strike literally knocked her off her feet and sent her crashing to the floor with a heavy thud. She was out cold.

By the time Pauletta came to, she was handcuffed and being loaded into an ambulance. When she turned her bloodied head, she saw Vince being lifted into another ambulance and Rozalla was right by his side. With all the commotion, Pauletta never heard Carmen slip in the back door. She never saw Lisa outside on the phone with 911. Her masterplan to get rid of everyone and ride off into the sunset had literally blown up in her face. Everything she'd done was in vain. Hiring Ashton to kill Kirsten, placing all the gasoline in Rozalla's car and on the side wall of the house was all for nothing. There would be no massive fire to kill Rozalla and her friends, no great escape for her and Vince. There would be no happily ever after for Pauletta.

EPILOGUE

Six months had passed since Vince was shot. Thankfully, the bullet had passed straight through his shoulder without hitting any major arteries. It had taken a little time for everyone to mentally process and move past the hell that Pauletta had brought to their lives. But move on was exactly what they'd done.

The sun was shining, the birds were singing and everyone was in a celebratory mood. Rozalla and Vince's daughters and closest friends had assembled at the chapel to watch them renew their vows. The ceremony was beautiful and by the time the happy couple finished declaring their love for one another, there wasn't a dry eye left in the building. Carmen and Lisa looked on, both knowing that this was the kind of love worth fighting for. Kirsten thought it was worth taking that bullet for. It was the kind of love they wanted for themselves.

After the ceremony the party was moved to a small reception hall. Everyone feasted on southern cuisine while the DJ played the old school music that Rozalla and Vince grew up on and fell in love to. Everyone laughed, danced, and raised their glasses to the happy couple that had endured so much.

Pauletta still dreamt of a life with Vince. She fantasized about him every day and talked about him as if he were her husband. She'd tell her stories of make believe to the other inmates in Central State Hospital, Georgia's largest mental asylum. She's been found mentally incompetent to stand trial and ordered to the asylum until she was found to be mentally stable. But Heather, she was completely sane and lost her job for sharing Rozalla's information with Pauletta. She tried to deny playing any role in all the mess that happened, but Pauletta's ramblings led authorities straight to Heather. She wasn't found criminally negligent, but had completely destroyed the successful career she'd built for herself. There wasn't another healthcare organization in the southeast willing to hire her.

Those that needed to be punished were, those that needed to forgive did, those that needed to be forgiven were, and love prevailed over all.